[d i g i t a l]

CINEMATOGRAPHY
& DIRECTING

CONTENTS AT A GLANCE

To create 3D digital content, you need more than just good lighting, textures, and modeling. If you want your 3D images and animations to be the best possible, you need to learn the art and technique of the camera within your 3D application. *[digital] Cinematography & Directing* was written for the 3D animator who wants to maximize the use of camera techniques with minimal struggle. Through the planning, pre-production, and storyboards detailed in this book, you'll be on your way to realizing your cinematic vision. Learn how to apply real-world camera principles to your 3D camera, and flesh out your knowledge by exploring the intricacies of rendering, editing, and sound.

[d i g i t a l]
CINEMATOGRAPHY
& DIRECTING

DAN ABLAN

New Riders

1249 Eighth Street, Berkeley, California 94710
An Imprint of Peachpit, A Division of Pearson Education

[DIGITAL] CINEMATOGRAPHY & DIRECTING

International Standard Book Number: 0-7357-1258-1

Library of Congress Catalog Card Number: 2001099383

Printed in the United States of America

First printing: November 2002

05   7 6 5 4 3 2

TRADEMARKS

WARNING AND DISCLAIMER

Publisher
David Dwyer

Associate Publisher
Stephanie Wall

Editor in Chief
Chris Nelson

Production Manager
Gina Kanouse

Managing Editor
Sarah Kearns

Acquisitions Editor
Jody Kennen

Senior Marketing Manager
Tammy Detrich

Publicity Manager
Susan Nixon

Project Editor
Jake McFarland

Copy Editor
Linda Laflamme

Indexer
Cheryl Lenser

Proofreader
Kelley Thornton

Compositor
Kim Scott

Manufacturing Coordinator
Jim Conway

Cover Designer
Aren Howell

For my family.

TABLE OF CONTENTS

ABOUT THE AUTHOR

 **Dan Ablan** has been involved in the visual arts for more than 20 years. He has worked as photographer, editor, producer, and 3D artist. Currently, Dan is the president of AGA Digital Studios, Inc., located in the Chicago area. AGA Digital Studios, Inc. creates 3D animations and visual effects for film and television, in association with Post Meridian, LLC. Dan is also the author of five other books from New Riders: *LightWave Power Guide, Inside LightWave 3D, Inside LightWave [6], LightWave 6.5 Magic,* and *Inside LightWave 7.* Dan has written for *LightWave Pro Magazine, Video Toaster User, 3D Magazine, 3D World Magazine,* and *NewTek Pro Magazine.* Dan was a contributor to *After Effects 5.5 Magic,* and he was also the technical editor for Jeremy Birn's *[digital] Lighting & Rendering,* both from New Riders Publishing.

About the Technical Reviewers

These reviewers contributed their considerable hands-on expertise to the entire development process for *[digital] Cinematography & Directing*. As the book was being written, these dedicated professionals reviewed all the material for technical content, organization, and flow. Their feedback was critical to ensuring that *[digital] Cinematography & Directing* fits our readers' need for the highest-quality technical information.

Jack "Deuce" Bennett II is a freelance CGI artist, whose background is in physical special effects for motion pictures and television. Deuce has been working in the film industry his entire life, and has such movies as *Robocop*, *Lonesome Dove*, and *Jimmy Neutron: Boy Genius* to his credit, as well as TV shows like *Walker, Texas Ranger*. Deuce has been using computers since he was nine, and he started off writing his own graphic programs. He is a unique combination of physical knowledge and virtual know-how.

Alan Chan is a Technical Director at Sony Pictures Imageworks in Culver City, CA, where he served as Look Development Lead on Warner Brothers' *Harry Potter and the Sorcerer's Stone*. Prior to Imageworks, Alan was co-founder of Station X Studios, where he supervised projects such as Tom Clancy's *Netforce*, as well as commercial work for Chevy Blazer, Budweiser, and Dodge Ram. Prior to that, Alan worked at Digital Domain, where he served as part of the Digital Ship Team on James Cameron's *Titanic*.

Alan is currently working on shots for the second part of Peter Jackson's *Lord of The Rings* trilogy, *The Two Towers*.

Terrence "Tman" Masson has contributed to 17 major film projects as an Animator, Technical Director, and Digital and Visual Effects Supervisor over the past 12 years. He also put in stints at Digital Domain and Warner Brothers, as well as two tours at Industrial Light and Magic after early years spent doing graphic design, commercials, flying logos, large format, and game projects. Terrence's most recent film projects have included *Hook*, *The Star Wars Trilogy Special Edition*, *Spawn*, *Small Soldiers*, and *Star Wars Episode I: The Phantom Menace*. Terrence founded his own consulting company, Digital Fauxtography, in 1993. In 1995, he co-founded the Visual Effects Resource Center at **www.visualfx.com** (now VFXPro.com). Terrence has directed a few award-winning short animated films such as *Bunkie & BooBoo*, and he wrote the book *CG 101: A Computer Graphics Industry Reference* (published by New Riders). Most recently, Terrence has been concentrating on real-time graphics, including such games as *Bruce Lee* for Xbox and *SimCity4* for Maxis/Electronic Arts.

In his spare time (ha!), Terrence is a contributing writer to VFXPro.com, tours the world speaking on various visual effects and CG topics, and still manages the occasional freelance gig like getting the *South Park* animation technique started for television.

ACKNOWLEDGMENTS

I need to thank my friends at New Riders Publishing. After working with them for over six years, I only have the utmost respect for their talent and dedication to the graphics industry. As I watched the *[digital]* series of books grow each year, my photography and video experience kept coming to mind. When I approached New Riders with the idea to add a "camera" book to their popular *[digital]* series, they were very open, and I thank them for their encouragement and belief in me.

The *[digital]* series was created by industry great, George Maestri. Thank you George for creating such a great book series. Things have come a long way from that lunch we had in New Orleans so many years ago!

Thanks to NewTek, Inc., makers of LightWave 3D, Aura, and the Video Toaster. Discovering the world of 3D animation and digital video was enlightening back in 1989, but finding a way in would not have been possible without your products. Thank you Tim Jenison for brining the power to the people.

Jody Kennen at New Riders Publishing deserves a raise! She has tirelessly nagged me… uh, I mean supported me, during the creation of this book. Thank you Jody for keeping me going and reminding me of the deadlines. Without you, this would not have been completed—at least, not in any reasonable amount of time! Alongside Jody, I need to express my gratitude to Jake McFarland, Project Editor, and Linda Laflamme, Copy Editor. You two have really helped this book come together. Thanks so much for your comments and efforts.

Jack Bennett II has been a tremendous asset to this book as a technical editor. His expertise in film and television production has been an invaluable guide to this book. Thanks Jack, and thank your Dad, too! Terrence Masson was also a technical editor for this book. Terrence, your vast knowledge of the industry is greatly appreciated. I was fortunate enough to have an old friend hop on board as a technical editor late in the game. Alan Chan stepped up and proved to be a key player in our team by providing last minute details and informative comments. Thanks Alan!

Thank you to my terrific wife, Maria. Thank you for letting me work!

Finally, I put my hands together for you, the readers. Your support of my previous books does not go unnoticed, and I hope this book will help you enhance your digital skills even further.

TELL US WHAT YOU THINK

As the reader of this book, you are the most important critic and commentator. We value your opinion and want to know what we're doing right, what we could do better, what areas you'd like to see us publish in, and any other words of wisdom you're willing to pass our way.

When you contact us, please be sure to include this book's title, ISBN, and author, as well as your name and email address. We will carefully review your comments and share them with the author and editors who worked on the book.

Email: **errata@newriders.com**

[CHAPTER]

1

INTRODUCTION

I T'S A QUIET MID-WEEK afternoon. You've finished your client
work for the day. A fresh pot of coffee is ready as you start up your
favorite 3D application. Your goal is to build something more creative than your normal day-to-day work—something you can be
proud to put on your demo reel. You begin modeling, then apply
the surfaces. You create textures, and set up the lighting. Tweaking
and twisting the parameters just so, you render to see how your creation looks. Not bad—but you are never happy. So, as you continue
to create your masterpiece, you practice what you've learned, constantly enhancing textures, lighting, and motions. But what about
the camera? Sure, you set it in place and framed your shot, but did
you really think about your shot? Did you consider the camera as a
significant element of your magnum opus? Have you ever? You
should.

1.1 PERSPECTIVE

When you look at the cover of this book, your eye is pulled a mile
down the street. The perspective on this shot is forced and exagger-
ated to convey a point. This book is about perspective—your perspective in the digital world. Equally essential is attention to the
camera and its perspective. Many animators, however, often overlook
the camera or give it only minimal afterthought.

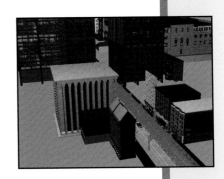

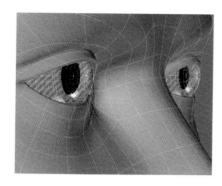

1.2 YOUR VISION

When working in 3D space, you have the ability to create whatever you can imagine. Your vision is as important to your work as the tools that you use, and knowing how to apply your vision to those tools is key to your success. This book will guide your perspective and your vision through the digital canvas. You will learn:

- How the camera works in a 3D world and how to translate real-world settings to the digital environment. (See Chapter 2, "The [digital] Camera.")

- The importance of storyboarding, visualization, and concept illustration. (See Chapter 3, "Storyboards," and Chapter 4, "Planning Shots.")

- How light affects the mood and tone of a shot and how to work with it effectively. (See Chapter 5, "Lighting.")

- All aspects of directing a shot: staging, angles, lines of action, and composition. (See Chapter 6, "[digital] Directing," Chapter 7, "Staging," and Chapter 8, "Lines of Action.")

"We must remember that a photograph can hold just as much as we put into it, and no one has ever approached the full possibilities of the medium."

—Ansel Adams

There are numerous elements to consider when creating 3D imagery, from lighting to textures to motions to cameras. The workflow you employ is up to you, and this book will not instruct you otherwise. What it will instruct you on is how to properly and creatively develop your eye so that you can visualize your shots before they happen. The pre-visualization you learn and practice will help determine your workflow in whichever program you choose.

1.3 TRADITIONAL ARTS

Many animators have backgrounds in the traditional arts, such as painting, drawing, or acting. It's often thought that the techniques used in these mediums are obsolete in the digital realm, but this couldn't be further from the truth. Think about it: The software you use was created based on real-world principles, so why wouldn't knowledge of traditional arts be useful when working with these programs? What's more, a background in photography or cinematography will *help* your digital creations. The traditional techniques of cinematography can all be applied in the digital world, as you'll see throughout this book.

If you are new to the digital world as well as the traditional arts, it's never too late to start. A trip down to the library or bookstore will yield a world full of information and ideas. Books, papers, and magazines that discuss and display real-world situations for photojournalists and film-makers can be your best friends when creating digital graphics. Use these resources to your advantage!

1.4 WHO SHOULD READ THIS BOOK

Anyone interested in improving their visual skills in the digital world can benefit from this book. You don't have to have a specific interest or background in cinematography or directing to work through these pages. Use this book if you are:

- Looking to enhance your creative skills and add that extra ingredient that your images and animations have been missing.

- A professional animator looking to improve your digital shots.

- A teacher needing a reference or ideas.

- A beginner or professional hobbyist wondering where to start when it comes to digital cinematography and directing elements in any 3D rendering software.

As with the other books in the *[digital]* series from New Riders Publishing, this book is written to be clear, not condescending, and to act as a reference and guide to your ever-growing creative skills.

1.5 SOFTWARE REQUIREMENTS

A clear advantage of the *[digital]* series is that you don't need a specific software application to work through these pages. *[digital] Cinematography & Directing* can guide you through any 3D application, as well as some 2D programs. These include, but are not limited to, the following:

- LightWave 3D (NewTek Inc.)

- Maya or Power Animator (Alias|Wavefront)

- Softimage XSI (Avid Technologies)

- 3ds max (Discreet)

- Strata 3D Pro (Strata Software)

- Houdini (Side Effects Software)

- Hash Animation Master (Hash Inc.)

- After Effects 5.5 (Adobe)

Because the software debates will continue for years to come, inevitably, it's the image that matters. What you create—which is why you're using the selected software in the first place—is what's important. In this book, it doesn't matter what software you use, because the X, Y, and Z axes don't change. Wide-angle shots remain wide-angle shots in any application. Such terms as "dolly," "pan," and "tilt" are the same if you're new to the industry or a seasoned pro. Although you can move the camera in 3D space in many 2D applications, such as Adobe's After Effects 5.5 and Eyeon Software's Digital Fusion, this book concentrates on the virtual camera in true 3D applications.

1.6 WHAT YOU SHOULD KNOW

The camera in your computer graphics application is not often the primary focus. In fact, it's the least thought of element in most animators' projects. I hope to change that. I started working in 3D because I couldn't achieve the shots I visualized and studied throughout college. As a student of photo and broadcast journalism, my main focus was the image, the picture. A picture is worth a thousand words? Not quite—a picture is endless. Perhaps I've been looking through a camera lens for too many years, but the ability to create any possible shot I can envision is an amazing thing.

"I am not interested in shooting new things—I am interested to see things new."

—Ernest Haas

The digital canvas that you and I work in can be overwhelming. When you run your favorite 3D application, you have the ability to create anything you can possibly imagine! Although textures, lighting, and motion are extremely important, you can very easily diminish or enhance the entire image you are creating simply by changing how it is seen. When you control a camera in 3D space, you are controlling how the audience will view the scene. You choose their point of view. And since point of view determines how an event is perceived, choosing a point of view is extremely important. Different shots and different points of view can change the way an audience will react to a scene. Point-of-view type shots such as wide shots, close ups, high angles, and more will be discussed throughout the book.

At one point in my career, I shot news for a CBS affiliate. There, I learned a few key things: Television news is no picnic, and, more importantly, the best photographers are editors, and the best editors are photographers. What this means is that even as you are shooting, even as you are setting up a shot, you need to be thinking about where you're going and the final outcome. You need to be thinking about the editing and post-production, and how your shots can be cut together. As you direct your subjects in the scene, you should be thinking not only about their dialogue and actions, but also how your direction will work when it's time to put it all together. Is there continuity? How's the composition? Will it make sense to the viewer?

1.7 THE PROJECT

This book was written not as a technical reference, but rather a real-world project guide. Clear examples are one step to learning, but this book goes further by having you follow along with a single project that ties it all together. You'll begin your project with planning, then storyboards, camera shots, editing, and later, rendering.

I want you to think about shots, camera motions, focus, composition, lighting, action, angles, continuity, editing, and even sound. It seems like a lot to manage on top of trying to perfect a character's walk or properly time a complex expression, but it's really not. Learning about these techniques will change your viewpoint. By understanding the elements that can make or break a shot, you'll soon "see" how digital cinematography and digital directing become second nature.

The goals of this book are to encourage, enlighten, and empower you to better cinematography and directing within a computer environment. Each chapter will discuss key elements that add up to one significant variable—your vision.

2

THE [DIGITAL] CAMERA

TITLING THIS BOOK was difficult. I wanted to call it *The Digital Camera*, but that would obviously lead to quite a bit of confusion. Today's ever-growing digital marketplace has branched to include digital photography, which continues to grow by leaps and bounds. The phrase "the digital camera" generally leads to one thought—digital photography.

This book is not about digital photography, although photographic and film principles are very important to digital cinematography. And, while carrying around a laptop that's running your favorite 3D application is possible, it's not quite the same thing as always having a camera around your neck. Perhaps you've taken an interest in photography, or maybe you like to critique movies and how they are filmed. Maybe during your last visit to the movie theater, you saw a few shots that felt uncomfortable, but you just couldn't put your finger on why. How does that all relate to working in computer animation? Good question! This book will answer those questions and many more. But first, you should understand how a real-world camera translates to the digital world.

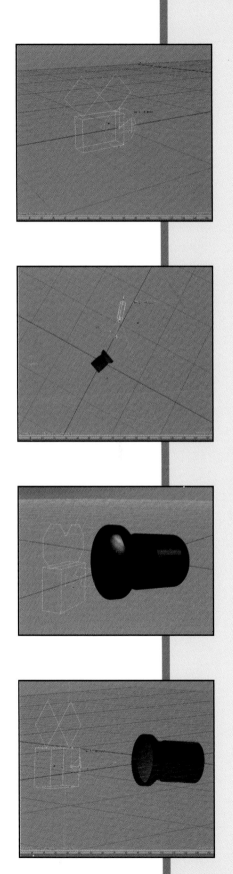

> "When you begin viewing the world through a camera lens, your senses sharpen as your mind and eyes are forced to focus on people and things never before noticed or thought about. I discovered that even if I didn't always take a picture, the simple act of carrying a camera and searching for something to photograph greatly sharpened my own powers of observation and allowed me to experience much more of life."
>
> —Kent Reno

2.1 THE REAL AND THE UNREAL

How would you describe the camera in your 3D application? It is digital, but is it a "digital camera" as you know it in the practical world? The best way to describe what it is, is to understand what it does. A real camera is often much like the "unreal" camera within your digital canvas. It can zoom, it can focus, and it can move in any direction you desire. Each type has advantages and disadvantages. You will find, however, that a digital camera offers an enormous range of control and flexibility. For example, the camera in your digital application can do just about anything you can imagine, such as rack-focus effects and shooting with extreme wide angles, fish-eye lenses, or telephoto lenses. What's even cooler is that your "digital" camera is devoid of wires, cables, and technicians! You can pan, swoop, twist, or spin the camera to your heart's content—without even paying union fees!

Just as a 3D artist trained in traditional painting has an advantage in the digital environment, the same goes for those with backgrounds in cinematography. But before you can use a camera in a 3D scene, take a look at how real-world principles translate to the digital world. This chapter will discuss:

- Aperture
- F-stops
- Focus
- Depth of field
- Aspect ratios and pixels
- Film and grain

The best place to start is with the most fundamental subjects: aperture and f-stops.

2.2 APERTURE AND F-STOPS

If you have experience in film or photography, you should certainly know about aperture. Simply put, the *aperture* is an opening, generally a circular hole or similar shape, within a camera lens that controls the amount of light coming into the camera and onto the film or computer chip. The aperture is controlled by *f-stops*. The "f" refers to the focal length of the lens divided by the aperture. Camera operators are always concerned about aperture and f-stops, as these can make or break a shot.

The aperture on a real camera is a mechanical diaphragm that operates like the iris of an eye (see Figure 2.1).

THE ORIGINS OF F-STOP

The origin of the lower case "f" in f-stop goes back to 1932 and renowned photographer Ansel Adams. He and a few others, Willard Van Dyke, Imogen Cunningham, Edward Weston, Hentry Swift, Sonya Noskowiak, and John Paul Edwards, formed a group called f.64. This group was dedicated to pure photography, including portraits and landscapes. Van Dyke originally proposed the name US256, but Adams thought it sounded like a highway. He simply wrote an "f" and then put a dot similar to the old aperture settings. They soon updated this to an f with a slash mark to read Group f/64.

The "f" in f-stop is a number or value that represents the ratio between the size of the focal length of the lens to the aperture. The "stop" portion of an f-stop is determined by a division of a lens' focal length and the aperture's diameter. This division is in millimeters. An example might be a 50mm lens with an aperture of 25mm in diameter; the f-stop is f2.

When you talk about f-stops, no matter what the measurement, the same measurement of light is reaching the film or digital chip. When a change in f-stop occurs, the light is either doubled or cut in half.

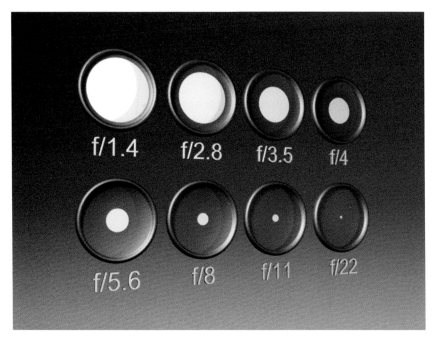

2.1 An aperture on a camera lens works like the iris of your eye, opening and closing to allow more or less light into the camera.

If this diaphragm is open wide, you have a low f-stop, which allows more light into the camera. Conversely, an aperture that is small (the diaphragm is closed to a tight opening) is a high f-stop, allowing very little light into the camera. It's confusing at first, but just think opposites:

- Low f-stop, more light (larger lens opening)
- High f-stop, less light (smaller lens opening)

NOTE

In addition to aperture and f-stops, real-world photographers also have to consider shutter speed and film speed. Think of the shutter as the eyelid of the aperture (the iris). When a photographer pushes the button on a camera to take a picture, the shutter opens and closes quickly, exposing either film or a digital chip to the amount of light specified by the aperture opening. Shutter speeds are measured in fractions of seconds, such as 1/30 sec or 1/125 sec. Higher shutter speeds are used for fast-moving action, such as sports. Lower shutter speeds are used for shots with less movement. Generally, you don't have to worry about shutter speed when working in the digital 3D environment. However, you may consider the animation frame rate to correspond to motion blur in 3D animation. Frame rates will be discussed more in detail in Chapter 10, "Resolutions, Compression, and Rendering."

T-Stops

Along the lines of f-stops are t-stops. Often thought of as the same thing as f-stops, t-stops are actually quite different. The "t" stands for *transmission* and is a "theoretically perfect" f-stop. However, because of intermediums like the glass lenses, f-stops are never actually perfect, and there is always a loss of light. A t-stop's numbers are always higher than f-stops. A t-stop factors in the loss of light from a camera lens's optics. While t-stops are not used too much in photography, they are used in filmmaking and scientific work for more accuracy.

Aperture indirectly plays a role in digital cinematography because many 3D applications include settings for f-stops. Varying f-stops in the digital environment directly play a role when applying depth of field effects.

The "stop" portion of f-stop comes from original photographic technology in which the aperture was selected by turning a wheel that had various sized holes. Each hole let in twice as much light as the previous hole. With this in mind, you can understand what it means when someone says to "stop down" your lens. You can think of f-stops in terms of your own eyes. When you squint, you decrease the opening (larger f-stop) and block light from entering. Or, if you want to see more, you open your eyes wide (smaller f-stop) and let more light in. F-stops can range anywhere from f/1.4 to f/28. The lower f-stop number is considered "shooting wide open," meaning the aperture is at its largest opening, allowing more light to enter the camera lens. The higher f-stop number closes the aperture, allowing less light into the camera (see Figure 2.2). F-numbers are ratios. An f-stop is the ratio between the focal length of the camera lens and the diameter of the diaphragm (aperture) opening. For instance, f/2 means that the aperture diameter is 1/2 the focal length of the lens.

So when do you allow more or less light into the camera and why? And how does the f-stop play a role? More importantly, why in the world is this important to digital cinematography? A basic understanding of photographic principles can help you assess your 3D situation in terms of both lighting and depth of field.

2.2 With a wide aperture set to f/2, the focus point is concentrated to a specific point. As the camera lens is stopped down to f/16, an increased depth of field is created. A typical 3D animation without depth of field turned on will always render everything in focus, similar to a small aperture like f/16 or higher.

2.3 DEPTH OF FIELD

One complaint in many 3D animations is that they look "too clean." So, what do you do? You can add more detailed textures, better lighting, softer shadows, and even radiosity. But watch any movie, and you'll see something not often put into 3D animations: *depth of field*. Planning a shot so that depth of field can be applied means properly setting up lights and cameras, as well as positioning subjects appropriately. Be sure to visit Chapter 7, "Staging."

Depth of field, often called DOF in computer software, can significantly change the look and feel of your shot. It can push the viewer's attention to specific subjects simply by changing the focal point. A large depth of field, often referred to as *deep focus*, keeps most everything in your shot clear and sharp (see Figure 2.3), while shallow depth of field leaves only a small area in focus, blurring what's in front and behind the subject (see Figure 2.4).

Depth of field is used in many animation settings, such as a subject focusing on a distant object. Or perhaps you have modeled and textured a small insect. When it's time to render, you want to create the most life-like image. If you shot the insect with a real camera, the area around the tiny object would be out of focus. A tight close-up creates a shallow depth of field, giving your digital shot added realism.

2.3 An image with a small diameter aperture (a high f/stop, such as f/18) provides a sharp focus throughout the image, both close and far from the camera lens. There is more depth of field in this shot.

2.4 An image with a large diameter aperture (a low f-stop, such as f/2.8) provides less (or shallow) depth of field. The objects before and after the point of focus appear blurred, calling specific attention to the subject.

The aperture controls not only the amount of light, but also the depth of field. The virtual camera in your 3D application often has its own aperture to match real-world settings. Although this digital version of a camera's diaphragm is merely a representation of an effect, the results can equal that of a real camera. You can use depth of field in a number of shots:

- Over the shoulder talking head shots
- Close-up objects
- Product shots
- Hand-held camera effects

And there are many more opportunities to add depth of field when creating 3D shots, which you'll see throughout this book. But are there times when you wouldn't want to have depth of field applied? Yes. Everything should be in focus for:

- Landscapes
- Group shots, such as product line-ups or crowd shots
- Cartoon or cel-shaded animations
- Aerial shots

Depth of field can also be animated, at least in the digital world. For example, many shots in movies and television use *rack-focus* shots. These are shots that changes focus over time, perhaps from one person talking to another. The cinematographer needs to manually adjust the focus, aperture, and any other settings on the fly while shooting the scene. In the digital world, it's much easier. You can assign a focus point to your 3D camera, set an appropriate f-stop, and then simply keyframe that focus point at any desired time. Deliberately repositioning your focus to create animated depth of field can greatly improve the look and feel of your animations.

2.4 LENSES AND FOCAL LENGTH

You can't really talk about apertures, f-stops, and depth of field without understanding a little more about lenses. Camera lenses vary greatly from brand to size, but they all have f-stops and perform the same function—they bring light into the camera. Film cameras and many new digital cameras have interchangeable lenses to change from wide-angle shots to telephoto. But in the digital world, you don't have to change lenses; instead, you change focal length and zoom factors. The focal length in most 3D applications equates to that of a real-world lens (see Figures 2.5–2.8). Although the values are not exactly accurate across the board, it's the focal length setting that will provide a wide-angle or telephoto look.

2.5 The SoftImage XSI camera panel offers specific presets for various types of lenses.

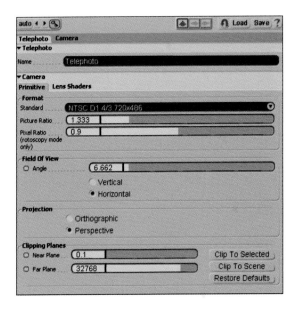

2.6 LightWave 3D 7.5's Camera panel offers a range of real-world settings to match camera lenses, as well as aperture.

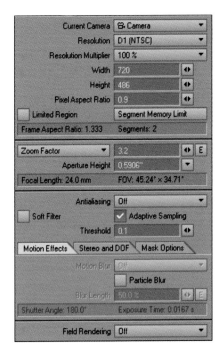

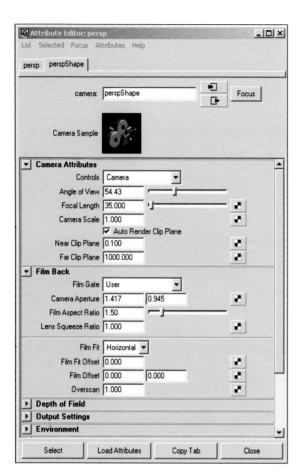

2.7 Maya's Camera panel also offers control over focal length and more.

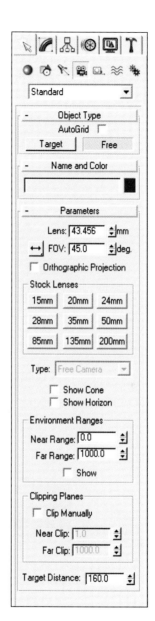

2.8 3ds max's camera works like a real-world camera, as do the other 3D applications.

Adobe's After Effects 5.5 offers real-world settings, but, surprisingly, is not a true 3D application. Figure 2.9 shows the After Effects Camera panel, where you can visually see the camera lens settings, as well as specific aperture settings.

2.9 The After Effects 5.5 Camera panel is one of the more intuitive control areas available in software applications.

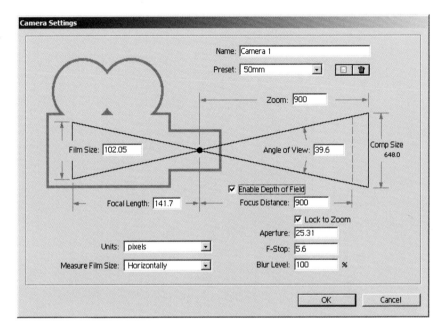

So what is focal length, and how does it work? *Focal length* is an optical term that means the distance, usually in millimeters, from the lens to the point of focus (the subject). The longer the focal length of a lens, the smaller its *field* or *angle of view*. Given that, a long telephoto lens, such as a 400mm, can view a small area only. This is not to be confused with how far the lens can see, only what it sees. For example, a camera lens with a 400mm focal length is twice as powerful, but has half the field of view, of a 200mm lens. On the flip side, a 20mm lens has a very wide angle of view (hence, it's called a *wide-angle lens*). You can very easily apply real-world camera lenses and focal lengths to your digital scenes simply by entering the desired values in your software application's camera control panel. (See Figures 2.10 and 2.11.) It's a lot easier than changing lenses!

In the digital environment, you can animate focal length to give your animation a very different look. This will be explained in detail in Chapter 6, "[digital] Directing."

2.10 In this 3D scene, the camera's focal length (its lens) was set to 120mm. You can see that the overall look is tight on a specific area of interest.

2.11 This is the same shot as the previous figure, but with the focal length set to a 35mm lens. The field of view is much wider.

Knowing when to use specific focal lengths is really up to you as a digital cinematographer. Choosing the right focal length, f-stop, and other camera settings is what a true cinematographer must decide for each production. As a 3D animator and digital cinematographer, you must decide when and how the right camera settings will be used. The project example throughout this book will be used to help you understand many different situations you can encounter.

2.5 ASPECT RATIOS

Just as depth of field and focal length define the image you're capturing, the aspect ratio defines the image's display. An *aspect ratio* simply describes the shape of the viewing screen by defining the relationship between a frame's width and height. The typical aspect ratio for television and video is 4:3, which is also called 1.33:1 in cinematic circles (see Figure 2.12). The first number (4) refers to the screen's width, and the second (3), its height. Film in theaters is shown at 16:9 aspect ratio, also described as 1.78:1 (see Figure 2.13). Now, high-definition television sets (HDTV) are bringing the 16:9 ratio into our homes (see Figure 2.14).

2.12 Most television is shown in a 4:3 aspect ratio, while films in theaters are shown at 16:9. Although still rectangular, a 4:3 ratio is closer to a square screen shape than a 16:9 ratio.

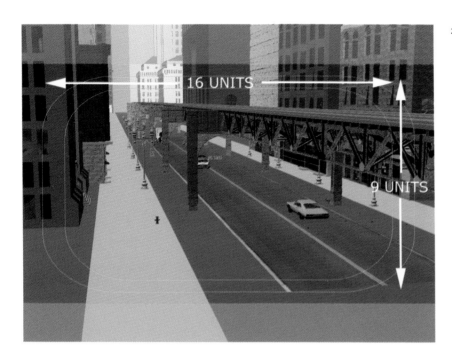

2.13 The 16:9 ratio, sometimes referred to as "letterboxed," is used most often for film.

2.14 1.78:1, or 16:9, is the aspect ratio of new HDTV and wide-screen televisions, as well as many films.

How did these aspect ratios become the standard? When the first moving images were put on film, 4:3 was used, and it became the Academy Standard Aspect Ratio (see Figure 2.15). This aspect ratio remained until the 1950s, when wide-screen (16:9) aspect ratios emerged. In the '50s, television became immensely popular, and filmmakers needed a way to get people back to the movie theaters. By using an aspect ratio that was twice as wide as it was tall (2.35:1), they created a new cinematic experience. When an image extends to fill more of your peripheral vision, what you're watching is more engaging.

NOTE

Most films released are kept to a safe 16:9 area, but their actual aspect ratios are 1.85:1 or higher.

2.15 The 1.33:1 or 4:3 ratio was common in the early days of film.

Today, cinematographers use aspect ratios of 1.33:1, 1.37:1, 1.66:1, 1.78:1, 1.85:1, and 2.35:1. Each ratio is increasingly wider, and which you use is often determined by film stock, such as a large 70mm, or the type of production. The cinematographer must decide which aspect ratio works best for the budget and the overall look of the film. As a digital cinematographer, you have the freedom to experiment and mimic any of these real-world aspect ratios in your animation work.

2.6 THE NEXT STEP

This chapter took you on a not-so-technical journey of basic camera principles, all of which can be used in the digital realm. Before you begin setting up your 3D camera, however, you need something to shoot! And to shoot something, you must plan. Read on to learn how storyboards, concepts, and visualization can help you bring paper to pixels.

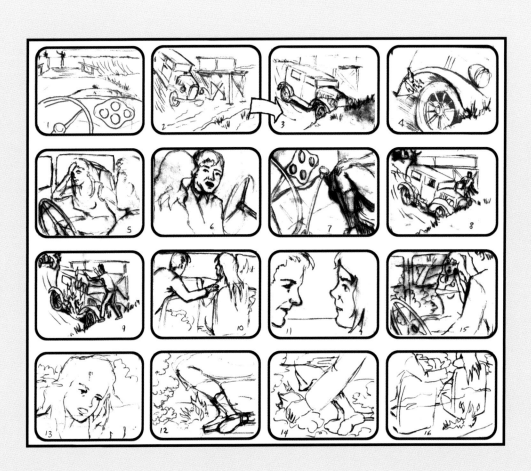

3

STORYBOARDS

W HEN YOU BEGIN A PROJECT, it usually starts on paper. Things as simple as going to the grocery store often begin with a grocery list written on a piece of paper. When we plan out these books, we first create an outline. By the same token, home renovations begin with a blueprint. So why would you start an animation project without the same sort of preparation?

Storyboards are blueprints for your digital content. Often only thought of for major motion pictures, storyboards can be useful even to the independent corporate animation creator. You'll find that employing storyboard techniques in your work can save you time and energy, especially when it comes to digital cinematography and directing. The production process, be it for film, video, or 3D animation, starts with a script, or even an outline. From there, planning can begin visually, which is where the storyboard comes in.

Planning and using storyboards may seem like more work, but only at first. Isn't just going ahead and starting your project the most direct approach to an end? Not always. In this chapter, you'll see how storyboarding can bring you closer to your vision by helping you prepare your shots, 3D models, levels of detail, and inevitably determine how you will direct the shots in your animation.

This chapter will help you think like both a cinematographer and a director. The director decides what each shot will be, while the cinematographer decides how those shots will look. For both of them, the process begins on paper.

3.1 FROM PAPER TO PIXELS

Planning is essential to every aspect of life: You plan your day, your finances, your schooling, your marriage, and so on. If you were preparing to make a movie, or even shoot a corporate video, you would plan your project on paper first, right? So why wouldn't you plan out your shots when working in the digital environment? Planning what you're going to do and how you're going to do it is the smart way to work. Work smarter, not harder.

If an animation project is the road and you are the driver, the storyboard is your map. Storyboards help you plan where you're going and guide you along the way, helping you avoid unwanted turns, which can cost you both time and money. Good storyboards help reduce the overall cost of a production as well, because the shots are planned out, leaving unnecessary shooting aside. You might think that unnecessary shots won't cost you any money because you are creating them on the computer. You're not building sets or hiring electricians like a film production company, of course. But *time* is money. Unnecessary shots mean that you, or your digital crew, need to build, texture, and set up additional models and sets. Computer time, machine time, and salaries still have to be paid—digital or otherwise. And if time is money, storyboards will save the digital artist as well as the traditional artist.

Finally, storyboards help the editor put the movie together. They serve not only as a road map for the artist, but the editor as well. The editor can use the storyboard to piece together the digital shots you've created, in the order you planned, without guesswork. The result is a production on time and on budget.

This chapter will concentrate on the proper usage, purpose, and value of the storyboard. You'll see how simply drawing out your ideas up front will save you time in the end. But before you start your own storyboards, take a look at some examples by Jack Bennett II. Jack and his father have worked in the film and television production industry for 35 years, on such programs as *Walker, Texas Ranger*; *Captain Ron*; *Robocop*; and *Lonesome Dove*. Figure 3.1 shows a typical storyboard Jack Bennett created for television. Through the clear illustrations, you can see the progression of the scene's action throughout an event.

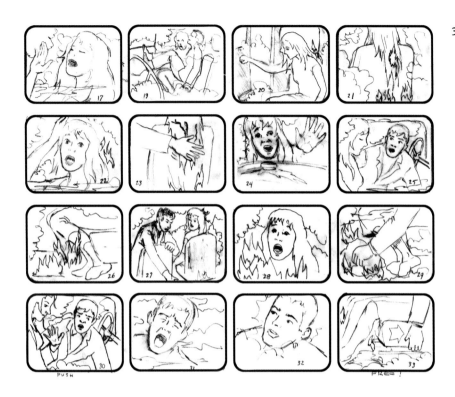

3.1 A typical storyboard for television. This process shows a beginning, middle, and end to complete a single scene.

This storyboard is just one way artists plan their shots. Here, you can see that an element of danger is present, involving fire and an automobile. A proper storyboard allows the director, actors, cinematographer, and effects people to prepare properly. From this point, the actors can rehearse their scenes. The lighting people can determine the best lighting situation, and the director can work out the shots.

Storyboarding is an art in itself. There are many people in the film industry whose sole job is creating storyboards. A storyboard artist can work with a director, screen writer, and cinematographer to develop the vision for a film. Most cinematographers and directors are storyboard artists in their own right, as well. So now you know how the pros use storyboards, but where should you begin? What are the first steps in creating this essential digital cinematic element? Start with a simple concept.

3.1.1 CONCEPTUAL ILLUSTRATION

Once a script is written, or at least to the point of a workable manuscript, the cinematographer or director sits down to plan out not only the shots, but also a vision for the production. Directors truly believe in thorough pre-production storyboarding. They pick up a pencil and paper and begin to flesh out their scenes. As an animator and visual artist, you need to be aware of your scene and your goal—and not necessarily in that order! In the digital realm, unless you're working on a large production, you are both cinematographer and director. This means that you are also the creative driving force that visualizes with storyboards. It's your job to bring the visual plan to the table.

On many levels, concept illustration is extremely important. It can establish a mood, production design, types of equipment needed for a shot, and more. In the digital environment, the storyboard can help you decide what type of digital camera lens to use, what model preparation you'll need, and what textures you'll need to acquire. To begin conceptualizing, you don't need to sit down and draw out your entire project or movie. Don't over-think it. Obviously, you have a vision of what you'd like to create, right? Start with that. It can be a simple as a rough sketch on a napkin or some scribble on the back on an envelope. The goal is that you get your ideas and visions out of your head and onto paper. For example, Figure 3.2 represents some basic ideas for the cover image of this book. The vision was in mind, but it needed to be brought to paper in order for the 3D modeling process to begin. To better understand how the creative visualization process should work, take a look at Figure 3.3.

3.2 At the start of a project, get your ideas on paper. The cover image for this book grew out of these two conceptual illustrations.

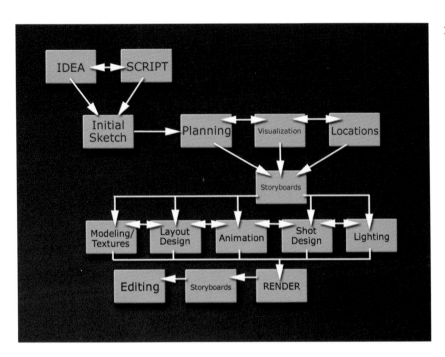

3.3 This diagram shows the process flow you should follow as you begin creating a feature-length movie, animation short, or even a broadcast identity package.

The conceptual flow for your projects, like all great things, starts with an idea. Take that idea, and visually enhance it, perfect it, and refine it. You can see from Figure 3.3 that the storyboard process is used more than once in a production workflow. It's used throughout, from planning to animating to editing. The storyboard feeds the animation process. Not only can you use storyboards to work out your shots, you can use them to decide what and how much detail to include in your 3D models. You can use them to help find the pacing of an animation while you work out which shots will take place.

3.1.2 PLANNING

Planning and visualizing your shots is the key to obtaining your goal. This requires concentration, thorough planning, and even location scouting. Perhaps your production resembles something of a real-world environment. Perhaps you want to re-create something that actually exists, such as Wabash Avenue in downtown Chicago. You can start with a few simple sketches, and then proceed to the location for even more detail. While on location, you might find things you hadn't visualized, such as stylized lampposts, alleyways, placement of trash receptacles, and more details that can add realism to your scenes. Conversely, you might find that your original vision does not match the real-world location. In either case, by going on location as part of your planning, you can work out any necessary cinematic and logistical details fully in your story-boards. Visiting locations also can help you decide how to direct shots later when actors are added to the mix. Figure 3.4 shows two photo-graphs used as reference for the cover of this book.

3.4 Planning out your storyboards can begin with real-world references. Here, two digital photos of the area reconstructed in 3D are used for "pre-vis." These shots will help plan the storyboards and the shots.

All of the resources you can include in the planning stages of production can help create the right storyboards. The right storyboards can help create the digital content you're envisioning. So how do you begin creating storyboards? What format do you use? What should be included?

3.2 THE STORYBOARDING PROCESS

Creating storyboards begins with a framed outline, generally in the aspect ratio you choose, such as 4:3 for television or 16:9 for film. It is important to decide which aspect ratio you'll use before creating storyboards, as the shot differences can be significant. Figure 3.5 shows a typical storyboard frame for video (4:3 ratio), and Figure 3.6 shows a typical frame for film (16:9 ratio).

4:3 Storyboard

3.5 If you're going to create storyboards for video or standard NTSC television, you can use a blank storyboard frame like this.

16:9 Storyboard

3.6 If your animation short is going to film, you might consider using a blank storyboard frame such as this. However, this frame size can be used for television or video as well.

NOTE

You'll be able to read more on aspect ratios and pixel resolution in Chapter 10, "Resolutions, Compression, and Rendering."

But picking the right aspect ratio is only one simple concern. Every storyboard frame you create represents one frame as seen through the camera's point of view. Your storyboards then should show action or movement. Figure 3.7 shows two storyboard frames showing the action of one sequence. As you can see, an arrow was drawn to more clearly identify the movement and pacing of the shot.

Often, time and budgets don't allow for complete storyboarding. So if storyboarding is essential to your production, how do you determine what to storyboard? Or, perhaps you simply want to flesh out some overall ideas rather than storyboard the entire project. What do you include? Consider what is important to the overall production:

- Locations and establishing shots
- Dialogue sequences
- Action sequences

The process of storyboarding for digital cinematography and directing is the same as it is for film and television, with some minor differences. Your storyboard in the digital world comprises mostly digital content or digital content composited with real world footage. Establishing shots, dialogue, and action sequences can be the pillars of your animation project, and, therefore, they are the key areas to storyboard. For example, many animation shorts start off establishing both a location and the characters involved. What drives your animation is the dialogue between characters and the action throughout. If you can storyboard through these three areas, you have enough to work with for both cinematic and directional purposes.

3.7 Two simple storyboard frames show the action of a sequence. Here, storyboards are used properly both to identify what is happening in the sequence and to determine the camera angle.

3.2.1 DRAWING

Learning to create storyboards also means knowing how to draw.
Regardless of your drawing ability, you can still create storyboards.
Drawings as simple as geometric shapes and even stick figures can
be enough for you to work out your shots. All you need is paper and
a pencil.

But perhaps you want to enhance your drawing skills so you can make
better storyboards and perhaps offer your services as a storyboard artist
as well as a digital content creator! If so, consider going to your local
library to study text on classic drawing, art, and still-life renderings.
Go one step further, and take a drawing class at your local college. This
is the great thing about digital content creation—your work can benefit
from all the references you acquire, from drawing classes to sculpture
to photography.

3.2.2 COMPOSITION AND FRAMING

The storyboard process outlines your production and presents the
opportunity to properly frame and compose your shot. A storyboard can
help you decide how the digital camera can move, pan, zoom, dolly, or
tilt in a particular scene. Figure 3.8 shows two storyboard frames with
good composition.

3.8 The right combination of framing and composition helps the continuity of the sequence.

The composition in Figure 3.8 works for a number of reasons:

- The first frame (labeled as frame 5) has the male character looking
  into the frame, while your focus is on the female. This shot allows
  the viewer to see the interaction between the two characters. You
  know to whom she is reacting.

- The headroom is not excessive, keeping your eye pointed to the
  main interest, the female.

- The second frame (labeled frame 6) is the opposite of the previous, with the female cheated left, looking into the frame. Your eye now focuses on the male and his dialogue. The shot is similar to the previous in that it keeps the viewer's attention on the character who's speaking, while not ignoring the character to whom he's talking. (When someone is cheated left, it simply means that the camera is panned to the right slightly. In this case, the camera being cheated left allows the female to look into the frame, making the shot more comfortable and aesthetic.)

Continuity is extremely important throughout your work and will be covered in detail in Chapter 8, "Lines of Action." Continuity helps the shots "work." That is to say, the proper composition and framing feed the continuity. Later in this book, in Chapters 6, 7, and 8, you'll be guided through a series of instructions that explains how to obtain the right framing, from camera angles, camera positions, the rule of thirds, and more.

3.2.3 STORYBOARD LAYOUT

If you're planning to become a professional storyboard artist, the layout you choose may be determined by the studio or director that hires you. Most likely, if you're reading this book, you're a "jack of all trades" and are storyboarding your own productions. If this is the case, you have the flexibility to layout the storyboard page any way that you choose. These suggestions, however, might help the process:

- Don't use a full sheet of paper for a single storyboard frame. As important as storyboarding is to your project, you don't want to spend all of your time drawing.

- Conversely, don't make your images too small. Putting too many storyboard frames on a single page makes them hard to see and inevitably defeats the purpose of a storyboard!

- Depending on your chosen aspect ratio, you can fit three or six storyboard frames on a page.

- Use 8.5×11-inch paper. You can use larger paper, such as 11×17 inches, but, the 8.5×11 size is nice because the pages can be organized neatly into binders. In addition, the 8.5×11 size is easier to photocopy.

Figure 3.9 shows a simple page layout using three storyboard frames with the 16:9 frame ratio on one 8.5×11 sheet of paper.

3.9 Three frames with the 16:9 ratio fit well on a 8.5×11-inch sheet of paper.

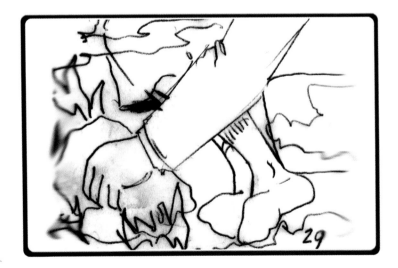

3.10 Six frames with the 4:3 ratio work well on a standard 8.5×11 page.

In Figure 3.10, you can clearly see that six frames with the 4:3 aspect ratio fill up the same-sized page well. But take a closer look at the two images—do you notice anything in Figure 3.10? With six storyboard panes at the 4:3 ratio, there's no room for text! Depending on your shot or the complexity of your storyboard, you may elect not to have text next to your frames. In most cases, however, using a storyboard layout with room for text (as in Figure 3.11) is a very good way to work. You can see the frames, and you have more than enough room for shot descriptions and notes.

Creating a storyboard template is as easy as making some boxes and lines in your favorite imaging program. Add areas for scene information, then print and copy it. You can even go so far as having a pad of storyboard sheets created, so you can bring it with you to sketch ideas and take notes as they come to you.

Remember, the importance of the storyboard to you as a digital cinematographer and director is to create the outline for your animation. The storyboard image, and the associated text and notes you create on the page will guide you through your project. The layout you choose for your storyboards should be comfortable for your needs. Again, if you're working with a director or studio, they may require you to use a different format. In most cases, however, it's the image that's important.

Scene _____ Shot # _____

Location _____ Director _____

3.11 Using four frames in the 4:3 ratio on a standard page leaves room for notes.

3.2.4 EXTENDED FRAMES

You've seen a few variations on storyboard layouts, and for most animation projects, these frames work well. If you've ever heard the term "think outside the box," now is the time to do so. Don't let the storyboard frame box you in (pun intended). Using extended frames, you can convey panning shots, tilts, or tracking shots. Think of an extended frame like this: Your shot might require you to pan across a specific area, and drawing just that area does not allow the storyboard to convey where the shot is going. By creating extended frames, the director and cinematographer can gain a sense of how a shot will move and flow. By the same token, extended frames allow you to show how subjects might enter or leave a frame, such as a man running from a mob boss down a city street. The extended frame gives the cinematographer and director extended visualization of a particular shot.

Creating extended frame storyboards is simple, as long as you ask two questions:

- Where are you starting your shot?
- Where are you stopping your shot?

Visualizing your shot is key to creating an extended frame storyboard. Take a look at Figure 3.12. Here you can see a three-frame storyboard shot displaying a panning shot across a colored drawing.

Using extended frames for storyboarding is often essential to describing the camera motion in a shot. In Figure 3.12, the simple sketch represents the shot, and the outlined box represents the camera. The arrows on each frame give the necessary direction to the cinematographer. This same approach can be used to describe a push or a pull of the camera in a shot. Once you read more about different camera styles and types of direction in Chapter 6, "[digital] Directing," you can utilize that knowledge in your storyboard creations.

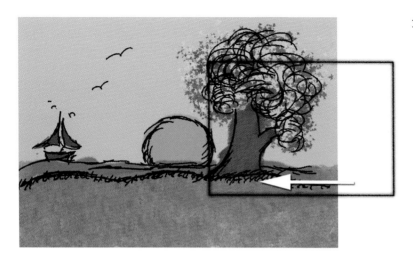

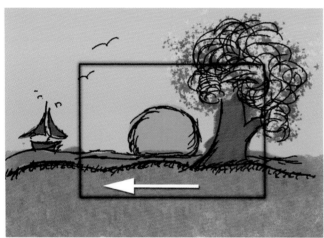

3.12 In this shot, a large area is drawn. On top of that is an outlined box representing what the camera will see. By showing the extended frame, the cinematographer and director can see ahead of time what the scene or shot entails.

3.2.5 OVERHEAD FRAMING

Sometimes your animation projects might include a good amount of camera movement, changing of cameras, or interaction between characters. In addition, there may often be a series of events that needs to be diagrammed as a whole before each individual shot can be storyboarded. Overhead framing is a useful technique for traditional filmmakers as well as digital ones. Overhead framing is probably something you've already done. Have you ever drawn out a map of directions for someone? You probably drew boxes that represented a few key landmarks, then proceeded to draw lines explaining which way to go—or better, which direction to take. Along these lines, overhead framing for your animation can be used for placement of characters, cameras, lights, or props. Most storyboarding is done from the camera's point of view, but you can storyboard out shots from a third-party perspective overhead, as in Figure 3.13.

In the digital world, you have an advantage over the traditional filmmaker in that you can build your virtual environment and work from computer screen grabs. Traditional filmmakers need to draw everything in the shot to plan out their actions. A view from above in the Y-axis can be used in combination with arrows and markers to describe a series of events, such as camera movement and vehicle direction.

3.13 Overhead framing is useful to plan movement and placement of both cameras and subjects.

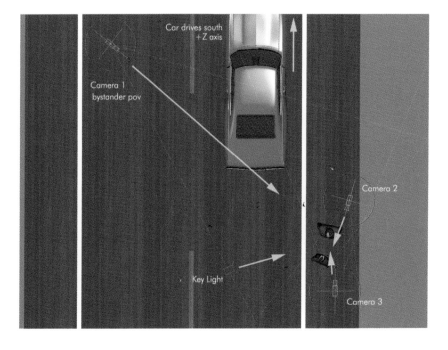

Overhead framing is also beneficial for working through important lines of action when there is dialogue between characters in a shot. Chapter 6, "[digital] Directing," will guide you through specific types of shots you can employ in your 3D environment.

3.3 THE NEXT STEP

Storyboards should not be a hindrance to your production, nor should they be a burden. Storyboards have significant value to you, your staff, and your entire project. Top directors believe in thorough pre-production storyboarding. Good storyboards can reduce the overall cost of a production—animated or traditional—because they prevent unnecessary set building and labor costs. Storyboards also serve the editor at the end of the production process by providing a roadmap of the shot order.

This chapter introduced you to storyboards and explained their purpose and value to digital cinematography and directing. While there are many facets to the storyboard process and varying approaches to technique, you can simply begin with a sketch. Here are a few things to remember in the preproduction storyboard process:

- Flesh out your ideas on paper.

- Design your shots.

- Work out the action.

- Plan what the camera will do, where it will start, and where it will end.

- Decide if the camera will zoom, pan, or tilt.

- Refine your ideas, and continue creating.

If you'd like to do more with storyboards, there are a number of excellent resources that can teach you to become a professional storyboard artist. Two such resources are *From Word to Image* by Marcie Begleiter (Michael Weise Publishing, ISBN 0-941188-28-0) and *Storyboarding 101* by James O. Fraioli (Michael Weise Publishing, ISBN 0-941188-25-6). In addition, you can use the vast resources of your local library or bookstore to learn more about drawing. Increasing any of your traditional art skills will always benefit you in the digital world.

Once you've created storyboards, the next step in your cinematic and directorial efforts is to plan your shots.

4

PLANNING SHOTS

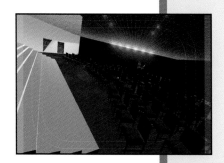

U NDERSTANDING AND KNOWING where you are going generally makes life a lot easier. Of course, many things in life are out of your control—but not in the digital world. In the digital realm, you do have control, and you should take full advantage of it. This chapter will help you do that by teaching you how to plan shots and work out what the virtual camera will see. You'll learn about the power you have up front to organize and prepare your digital shots.

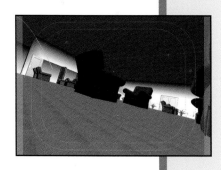

Planning requires you to use your creative visualization and foresight, while training yourself to think like a filmmaker. Your 3D animation software is a virtual multimillion dollar production studio. With it, you can create the world's greatest films. You control the sets, the weather, the lights, the camera, art direction, and even the talent. The common project you see throughout this book takes place underneath an elevated train in downtown Chicago. The focus of this project takes place all within one location. You might think that planning shots for just one set is not a big deal, but it is just as important—if not more important—than planning shots for multiple locations. The reason for this is because it can be very easy to confuse the viewer if shots do not flow and are not thought out. But before you let all this power go to your head, read through this chapter and learn to change your way of thinking from an animator and digital artist to that of an award-winning filmmaker.

"You've got to be careful if you don't know where you're going, because you might not get there."

—Yogi Berra

4.1 THINKING LIKE A FILMMAKER

So how do you make that mind shift? You're not a filmmaker, you are an animator. Yes, but not *only* an animator. You are the entire creative force behind the production at hand. You are the one who makes it happen, so you need to know more than just how to model, texture, light, and render. You need to think of the big picture, the schedules, the sets, the story—just like a filmmaker does. (See Figure 4.1.)

Part of this thought process is planning. To think like a filmmaker, you start with a story.

4.1.1 THE STORY

Regardless of what any advertising agency, publicist, or marketing firm tells you, the number one, most important aspect of any film—digital or otherwise—is the story. Working as a digital filmmaker, your first and foremost goal should be obtaining, understanding, and developing a story. (See Figure 4.2.)

4.1 It helps to think of the big picture when planning your shots. An establishing shot such as this lets viewers know where they are when the action begins.

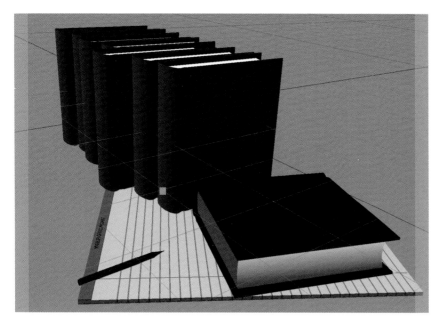

4.2 The most important planning stage is the story—without it, your animation has no legs, nothing to stand on.

The story is the backbone of any production. With a story, you can put everything in place, from sets, to models, voice talents, styles, and more. So what should you, the virtual filmmaker/cinematographer/director/animator, do to get the story?

- Network with friends or coworkers to come up with a script. Brainstorm often!

- Develop a script from the public domain. There are a great number of stories out there that are royalty free, waiting to be cleverly animated. You can find more about public domain stories (and music) here:

  http://www.unc.edu/~unclng/public-d.htm
  http://www.englishhistory.net/tudor/art.html
  http://www.utsystem.edu/ogc/intellectualproperty/image.htm

- Purchase the rights from a publisher to a book you think would make a good animated move.

- Write one yourself!

Thinking like a filmmaker means thinking of what a story is about, where you can get it, who will write it, and so on. Be sure to check the books at your local library about becoming a storyteller.

"Plans are worthless. Planning is essential."

—Dwight D. Eisenhower

RESEARCH

Once a story has been created, bought, or otherwise obtained, it's time to sit down and do your research. (See Figure 4.3.) Perhaps your story takes place in the late 1800s in upper New York state. Life in the late nineteenth century was very different even from that of the early twentieth, and your story should be accurate to its period. For example, think of the clothing, housewares, homes, even dialogue that matches the story's time. As a filmmaker, you need to explore these points. No matter what the time period of your story, proper research is vital.

If your story takes place in the future, do you still need research? You bet you do! You can research scientific data which can be translated to your needs for more accurate-sounding dialogue. You can research what other filmmakers have done with movies or shorts on the same subject matter so your project can stand alone.

Research can go on throughout a production, but essentially it's done up front. For example, you can be researching while the storyboard artist is working out the shot list. The Internet is an outstanding resource for researching your story. The proper research can help you in the digital world by providing reference photos or drawings for proper modeling and texturing. Research can help determine lighting conditions as well.

4.3 Research is essential to getting the details right.

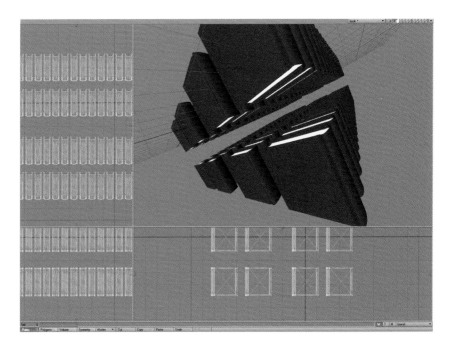

4.1.3   PRODUCTION DESIGN

Now that you're on the right track and thinking like a filmmaker, take a few moments to explore the importance of production design. (See Figure 4.4.)

4.4 A view of the set used to create an animation short. There are many ways to shoot within this environment.

Although most 3D animators don't think of production design as part of the creation process, most filmmakers do. As a top-notch digital cinematographer and animator, you know that production design is a key element in the planning stage of any production. So what is production design, and how does it translate to the digital content creation universe you live in? Production design involves:

- Creating set designs
- Establishing color schemes
- Deciding on costume design
- Establishing locations
- Deciding what props are needed

Production design is the overall visual appearance of a movie. In film-making, the production designer is responsible for creating the style of the production, as well as establishing and planning the visual design. This job is a very creative role and a key position in the production team. Production designers are involved from the beginning of the production process, and most of their work is considered "pre-production." A production designer develops the initial design concept for a production and works very closely with the director, art director, and costume designer. The production designer generally hires the art department and art director, creates detailed designs, and establishes the work that the art department will do. The production designer is also responsible for making sure the vision and initial design is realized.

As a digital production designer working in 3D animation, you may have a slightly easier job than traditional production designers. But the areas of concentration remain the same. This is because you are not limited by construction and the costs associated with it or by lighting limitations or physical impossibilities.

4.1.4 LIGHTING SITUATIONS

Lighting is often left to the gaffer on a movie set. As you've already figured out, you are your own gaffer when creating 3D animations. Lighting can be one of the most rewarding aspects of digital cinematography, as it can change the mood, feeling, and interpretation of any shot. (See Figure 4.5.) Thinking like a filmmaker, you need to consider the lighting conditions for your story and your overall project.

Lighting for digital cinematography is certainly different than in traditional film and video. This can be both a benefit and a hindrance. It's a benefit because you have complete control to put lights exactly where you want them. But it can be a hindrance because in traditional movie making, the filmmaker may rely on natural light for that perfect shot—a look that is often difficult—almost impossible—to reproduce in the computer.

Chapter 5, "Lighting," will guide you through the various types of lighting so you can create the specific look you're after.

4.5 Lighting is essential to digital cinematography.

4.1.5 SET DESIGN

Set design is just as important as research for digital filmmakers, although digital artists often do not think they are responsible for it. Thinking like a filmmaker means thinking of *all* aspects of the production, including set design. The research you do will help determine the set design. Here's an example: Your project takes place in the 1950s. You've done your research, searched the Internet, and have files full of pictures, newspaper clippings, magazine articles, and news footage. You can take bits and pieces of this research to create your set. (See Figure 4.6.)

Robert Zemekis took people back in time in *Back to the Future*. Although the film was shot on the Universal Studios back lot in 1985, Zemekis transformed the set into 1955 through signs, cars, lampposts, storefronts, and so on. The viewer has to believe in what the filmmaker is selling, and in this case, it was 1955. As a digital content creator, you have an advantage over traditional filmmakers because you can add to the set design very easily. Just model, texture, and place elements in at will. You don't need a producer's approval (in most cases), and a digital prop often is much less costly than a real one.

4.6 Mixed media placed within a frame are planned and arranged well for a comfortable-looking shot. (Rob Maxwell, **www.3drst.com/ robertmaxwell/**.)

4.1.6 THE CAMERA

Thinking like a filmmaker means thinking visually, as if you're looking through a camera lens. Visualize your shots, plan what you want the camera to see, and plan what you want your viewers to see. (See Figure 4.7.) The camera is the digital eye, and it's one of the most exciting aspects of digital content creation. You can make the camera see anything you want and go anywhere you desire. When it comes to the camera, you need to think like both a filmmaker and an animator. As discussed in Chapter 2, "The [digital] Camera," you have an advantage over the traditional filmmaker; you have no film stock to worry about, no cables, no rigs, no tripods. Chapter 8, "Lines of Action," will guide you through the many variations of camera angles you can create in the computer.

A filmmaker decides in which aspect ratios a film should be shot and which lenses to use. The filmmaker discusses the ideas with the cinematographer, and with the right combination of efforts, a film can be made.

4.7 Planning your animation includes, of course, thinking about camera angles, but it also includes planning how many and what type of cameras you'll use.

4.2 THINKING LIKE AN EDITOR

A filmmaker thinks through the entire process of creating a movie. That movie can be a three-minute music video, a one-minute film for the web, or a feature-length release shown in theaters. Whatever the case, the filmmaker plans the movie from research to cameras to editing and audio. (See Figure 4.8.)

4.8 Animators use programs like Adobe Premiere to tie audio to their rendered creations.

The editing process is crucial to the entire film. Although it is done at the end of a production, you need to think about it throughout a project. Knowing what, when, and how an edit will happen in a particular sequence will help you create the right shot. Although it's a favorite expression of inexperienced producers, "We'll fix it in editing" is no way to create a movie, whether it's 1 or 100 minutes long.

Thinking like an filmmaker enables you to plan your shots, while thinking like an editor enables you to envision how those shots will come together. You'll learn more about the editing process and its importance in Chapter 11, "Editing."

4.3 AESTHETICS

Whether in the digital or traditional realm, a large part of deciding on an overall production design and planning your shots is aesthetics. Aesthetics, by definition, is a guiding principle in matters of artistic beauty and taste; it's the artistic sensibility that guides the production designer and director in setting the look and feel of a film.

Aesthetics are not something you automatically pick up on, but your eye senses it. Planning your shots means always thinking about the aesthetic value. Don't think of how a shot *looks*—how does the shot *feel*? For example, compare Figures 4.9 and 4.10, which are two shots of the same scene. Figure 4.9 is uncomfortable and awkward. Figure 4.10 is aesthetically pleasing to the eye. Figure 4.9 is uncomfortable to the eye because you don't know what you're supposed to be looking at. What's the character doing? Where is he looking? It's a bad angle, and the shot does nothing for the story. On the flipside, Figure 4.10 is lower and over the character's shoulder. The lighting is better, and you can see that the character is looking down the street. The shot is balanced and makes sense.

In the planning stages of an animation short, the father of a young boy who befriends a mob boss in Chicago goes looking for his son. Shot 4.9 wouldn't allow you to see that the father is searching, but 4.10 does. A long shot down an empty city street helps convey that the boy is nowhere to be found. The viewer gains a sense of the father's desperate, and perhaps futile, search.

4.9 A bad camera angle, inappropriate lighting with awkward shadows, and poorly placed characters create an uncomfortable shot that is not aesthetically pleasing.

4.10 A well-balanced shot, properly positioned characters, better light, and appropriate shadows create an aesthetically pleasing shot.

Planning your shots means thinking of all the elements that can make the shot work—and not work. Aesthetics can be anything in your shot that simply does not work, but some of the key ingredients to an aesthetically pleasing shot include:

- Proper, balanced lighting, including colored lighting and mood lighting, and the shadows the lighting produces.

- Proper framing of your shot.

- Appropriate staging throughout the scene.

- Proper direction of your shot.

These topics will be discussed in Chapter 5, "Lighting," Chapter 6, "[digital] Directing," and Chapter 7, "Staging."

The aesthetic value in your production does depend on the elements listed, but it also has a lot to do with your own personal style. Just like drawing, painting, or photography, 3D animation is an art form. (See Figure 4.11.)

4.11 3D artist Ted Domek (**www. teddomek.com**) has a unique style all his own. Here, a few simple shapes and creative lighting generate a completely different environment.

4.3.1 STYLE

Planning your shots requires knowledge of many cinematic principles, but that does not mean that your own personal style should be left to fend for itself! Your style is your trademark, and you shouldn't let anything stand in the way of that. Why do you think such filmmakers as D. W. Griffith, Alfred Hitchcock, and Stanley Kubrick made such a name for themselves? Each had an individual style that carried through to his films. Director Tim Burton has a style all his own, clearly shown in such movies as *Edward Scissorhands*, *Batman*, and *James and the Giant Peach*. Some people like his style, some don't, but one thing remains: It's *his* style. As a digital director, you have the power and control to develop and exercise your own unique style.

You don't choose a style, nor do you strive to create one. Planning your shots and presenting your story as you envision it brings your style to the table. (See Figure 4.12.) Develop your own style through experimentation, different ideas, and varying production designs.

It's often been said that there are no original ideas left, and on most levels, the statement is true. If you are hired to create a futuristic environment, many of the elements you design will be based on other futuristic designs you've already seen. Although they may not be in the forefront of your imagination, the styles and ideas that have made their way into your subconscience over the years will manifest themselves—one way or another. There's nothing wrong with that, but do your best to make the style of your digital animation all your own through planning, set design, research, and aesthetics.

> "Style is knowing who you are, what you want to say, and not giving a damn."
>
> —Gore Vidal

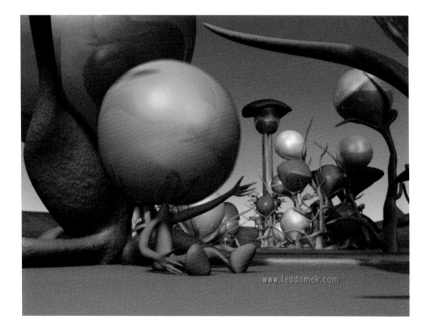

4.12 Low angles with similar shapes help bring this shot to life. Your eye wanders and finds many interesting things to look at in this unique style.

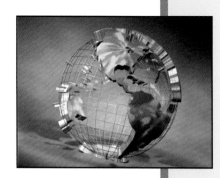

[CHAPTER] 5

LIGHTING

WHEN AN ANIMATOR THINKS about the work ahead with a new project, the thought process often involves work in stages—modeling, character rigging, texturing, lighting, camera placement, and rendering. A filmmaker thinks of the entire process at once. Light to the filmmaker is both a trouble and a blessing. It can be the cause of many problems that need to be solved, such as exposure, continuity, and lens reflections, but it can also be a benefit to the filmmakers because they can harness various lighting situations to create moods, feelings, or dramatic effects.

You, as a digital filmmaker, don't need to worry about many traditional light problems. In the digital world, there is no light until you create it. You are fortunate enough to have the tools to establish your own specific and consistent lighting conditions. You do, however, have one lighting limitation that traditional filmmakers do not: render time. The type of lighting you choose can make a significant impact on your render times and, hence, your production schedule.

This chapter will guide you through various lighting situations, cinematic uses, and how to use light as a tool in your production. It will also give you some basic information about types of lighting available in most of today's 3D animation programs.

"Vision, I say, is related to light itself."

—Galileo Galilei

5.1 GENERAL LIGHTING CONCEPTS

Light can be your best friend and worst enemy. Not only are you concentrating on the shot, the set, and the talent, you have to consider the light in every situation. Is it too hot? Is it too soft or too hard? Does it create the right mood and feeling? One of your foremost concerns when putting a shot together, light in your computer environment can be anything you make it. It can be any color, from any direction, with any intensity you desire. You can use *gobos*, or cookie cutter images, to shape your light. For example, if you cut a hole into a large metal plate, say, in the shape of a letter, you can put that plate in front of a light. When the light shines, it will be blocked except for where the hole in the plate is. The result is a light source cast in a specific shape. In 3D, creating gobos is as simple as making a black and white image (perhaps in Adobe Photoshop) and applying it to your light source within your animation program. With this same technique, you can project images (either still or moving) from your lights, or you can use negative lights to add darkness to an overly lit situation. You have every advantage at your finger tips—but what do you use when?

The scene at hand often will help dictate the type of lighting setup you should create. In addition, once you understand some general lighting concepts, it will be easier to decide what is appropriate lighting and what is over the top for your digital production.

5.1.1 FOOTCANDLES

Lighting inside your computer 3D environment doesn't really work in terms of footcandles. However, understanding this basic measurement of traditional lighting can help you assess your situation. A footcandle is a unit of measurement of the intensity of light falling on a surface, equal to one lumen per square foot. It was originally defined with reference to a standardized candle burning at one foot from a given surface. (See Figure 5.1.)

A footcandle is also a nonmetric unit of measurement for illumination, for example, 1 lumen per square foot. A lux then, is the international system unit of illumination, equal to one lumen per square meter. A lumen is the unit of luminous flux within that international system. It is equal to the amount of light given out through a solid angle by a single-candle source, which radiates equally in all directions. Lumens are units of illumination among a unit area of a spherical surface. You may have heard the term "lumens" when discussing video projectors. A common value would be 800 or 1000 lumens. The higher the number, the

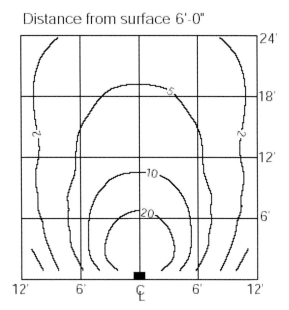

Distance from surface 6'-0"

5.1 This diagram shows a representation of one candle at the base. You can see the intensity falloff measured in feet.

brighter the light. The term luminous flux is the rate of flow of light per unit of time. What this all basically means is that to describe how bright a particular light source is, it's brightness can be measured based on direction, distance, and falloff. Understanding these principles will help you determine realistic light settings within your 3D environment.

In order to light a city street scene, it can be beneficial, if possible, to record the natural light settings in a similar real-world environment. How bright is the light above the buildings? How much light is reflected? Real-world settings can be matched within the computer for added realism and accuracy.

Photographers and cinematographers use hand-held light meters to measure the lighting conditions. Light meters measure light at one time, instantly. Understanding the brightness of a footcandle will help you understand lighting for different environments. At about 125 footcandles, your general office lighting makes it easy to read, but is not too bright for seeing your computer monitor. A television viewing room is usually lit at about 25 footcandles. Sunlight through an open window is roughly 600 to 800 footcandles. Outside, on an average sunny day, the footcandle measurement is 10,000. On a very clear and dry summer day, the sun can generate as much as 50,000 footcandles. Animators know that out-door lighting situations are brighter than indoor, but many do not realize quite how much. (See Figures 5.2 and 5.3.)

5.2 Knowing how bright the outside sun really can be will help you create outdoor 3D renders for projects such as architecture.

5.3 Interior lighting is much different from outdoor lighting, both in terms of brightness and color.

The question, then, is how do footcandles, lux, and lumens translate to your daily 3D animation work?

Light and how it is measured and translated in the traditional world is important to your knowledge base as a 3D animator, cinematographer, and director. It is important because these real-world principles are what create the mood, the look, and the feel of classic cinematic pictures. These lighting variables are the elements that you will emulate in the digital environment.

5.1.2 KELVIN

Lighting can be tricky, and some of the toughest jobs in the digital domain are those pertaining to lighting and rendering. They are tough because more often than not, lighting needs to match a real-world setting for compositing. Lighting has to make a rendering look as if it were shot outdoors, or it has to match interior lighting. Not only does the light's quantity have to match its real-world counterpart, the light's *quality* must be realistic as well. *Kelvin* is a qualitative measurement that you can use to match real-world lighting situations. (See Figure 5.4.) It's important to understand that footcandles, lux, and lumens are *quantitative* values. Because Kelvin, on the other hand, is qualitative, you can't directly convert footcandles, lux, or lumens to Kelvin.

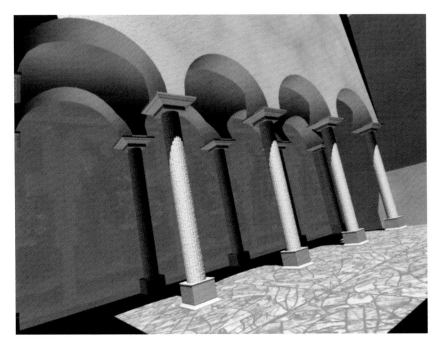

5.4 Outdoor daylight is very bright, obviously. You need to remember this when creating daylight 3D scenes.

5.500K
Daylight

4,200K
Cool White
Fluorescent

4,000K
Clear White

3,200K
Warm White

3,000K
Halogen

2,700K
Incandescent
Indoor

2,200K
Dim, warm

5.5 Kelvin temperatures represent changes in the color of light. As the value increases, the color changes accordingly.

Kelvin is a measurement of the color temperature of light. It is the color of a light source's output in relation to the degree of heat generated, which produces a specific color of light. Daylight, for example, is roughly 5500 degrees Kelvin. Figure 5.5 shows how varying Kelvin temperatures represent different colors of light.

> **NOTE**
>
> Lumens, lux, and footcandles are quantitative in measurement. Kelvin is a measurement of light temperature and is qualitative.

The visible light around you is the light that lies between the wave lengths of ultraviolet and infrared. This light contains all colors of the rainbow, from reds to blues, as you can see from Figure 5.5. Color temperature is quantitatively measured in degrees Kelvin and can be indexed according to the light generated. For example, a reddish light is measured around 2000 degrees Kelvin and lower, where as blue light is 5000 degrees Kelvin and up.

Some 3D applications allow you to use Kelvin values as an input, such as NewTek's LightWave 3D. Figure 5.6 shows the Light Color selector in that program. Here you input the desired Kelvin temperature, then LightWave calculates the corresponding RGB light color.

Using Figure 5.5 as a reference, experiment with the Kelvin temperature settings in your chosen 3D application and test the results. Not all lights, however, need to be calculated with Kelvin temperatures when working in 3D. Ambient light is a perfect example.

5.6 3D animation packages, such as LightWave 3D (shown here), allow you to input Kelvin temperatures to determine light color values.

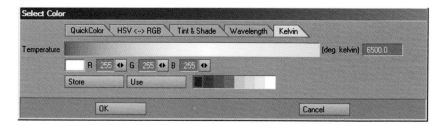

5.1.3 AMBIENT LIGHT

Ambient light refers to the illumination in areas not hit by direct light. For example, the area under a desk or the space behind an open door has ambient light. If you're indoors, any outside light, such as sunlight coming through windows or an overhead room light, can be considered ambient light. But be warned: Do not confuse sunlight with ambient light. To properly create sunlight, you need a directional light source that deliberately lights a specific subject or area. Ambient light is an area that many animators often overlook or at least leave to their program's default settings. Understanding how important this lighting is in your digital environment is important to the overall lighting quality of your scene.

Leaving the work to your program's defaults can do your scenes a disservice because ambient lighting is inconsistent and not often accurate in the digital environment. Ambient light by default in most 3D applications is too bright, leaving a flat, often boring, render. Figures 5.7 and 5.8 show the effects of too much ambient light and no ambient light.

The scene in Figure 5.7 attempts to focus the viewer's attention on the subject by using a single spot light to illuminate it. Your eye is supposed to focus on the watch, but too much ambient light makes your eye wander. Figure 5.8, on the other hand, has no ambient light. A single spotlight pulls your eye directly to the subject. Beyond the light's illumination is darkness, precisely the goal of the shot. This is the beauty of digital imaging: *You* control the situation without compromise. Throughout your digital lighting environment, it's vital that you control the ambient light. In general, ambient light is not good to use in computer graphics. On occasion, you can use ambient light in low settings to help slightly fill the darker areas not directly hit by a light source. The best way to work is to start in total darkness and add light when needed.

5.7 This scene has too much ambient light.

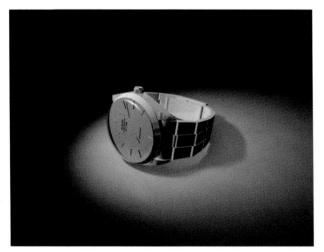

5.8 Eliminating ambient light from the scene focuses the viewer on the subject.

To know where more or less light is needed really depends on one thing—your eye. If your 3D environment appears too dark, it probably is. If you want more light to appear from above like a bright sun, position your sun above the subject and set up the light! Like anything in computer graphics, don't over-think it. If you want more light, add more light. If you want less ambient, create less ambient. You are in control.

5.1.4 LIGHT COLOR

So, if the best way to begin working is in total darkness (no ambient light), you're going to need more light! Ambient light helps add a slight color to scenes. For example, a bluish-green ambient value set low can help a daytime scene. The blue and green colors help represent bounced light from the sky and ground. However, larger amounts of ambient light create an artificial and unnatural overall general lighting, but no ambient light means that if you want to see something in your render, you'll need to add a light source. Light color plays a significant role in many aspects of 3D image creation. While this chapter can't discuss every possible situation, it can show you various conditions where colored lights are appropriate.

Take another look at Figure 5.8. This shot has a subject with one single spotlight above. The shot is dramatic and focused, but it could use a little more style and warmth. Cooler lighting is often done with blue or gray colored lights, which are great for nighttime or distance lighting. To make an image "warmer," orange or yellow lighting can be used. Warm colors tend to "pop" and come forward, drawing your eye, whereas cool colors tend to recede and blend. Warm and cool used together will compliment each other, creating a vibrant and interesting scene.

In everyday situations, what you see has the effects of many different colored lights. Most color comes indirectly from light bounced from different surfaces. Figure 5.9 shows the same render with one colored light set off to the right side of the frame.

Colored and tinted lights in your 3D environment can add depth, character, mood, warmth, and realism to your shots. They can add realism by simulating the look of bounced or reflected lights. (See Figure 5.10.)

5.9 Colored lights such as blue make an image cooler. Colored lights such as this are great for nighttime or creepy situations.

5.10 In this scene, the character is lit by a large main area light, simulating sunlight. A directional light beneath the character creates a simulated radiosity effect to give the appearance of bounced light. In the real world, light hits surfaces and becomes diffused within the surroundings. Snow is bright, and light hitting the surface bounces the white color up onto the character.

Colored lights do more than just add realism to a scene by replicating real-world situations. They also enable you to create specific styles throughout your work. Figure 5.11 shows an image rendered with a warm, deep, eggshell-colored light. The result is a soft, sepia-toned, dream-like image.

5.11 While you could always tint an image or animation after a render, changing lights within a scene while you render can produce various effects, such a soft, sepia-toned image.

Lights in the real world are colored—every one of them. The RGB spectrum of color combines together to create a white light. In the computer, colored lights, not often considered a general lighting practice, actually are very common. Beyond using colored lights to create a specific color or mood, colored lights are also symbolic. For example, traffic lights are red, glowing fire can use orange lights mixed with blue, and technical lights on equipment light up green. Use red lights as exit signs, or use a spinning orange light on the top of a tow truck. Figure 5.12 shows the cityscape scene from the book's cover in mid-daylight. Figure 5.13 shows the same shot lit for sunset, while Figure 5.14 shows a night-time view.

5.12 The cityscape scene from the book's cover is lit with general area lighting. A large, soft off-white light high above the scene creates lighting for midday. Although this image appears as if it's lit with white light, it's a light tinted with a soft yellow, simulating sunlight.

5.13 The same cityscape scene is now lit with a distant, general light tinted to a rich orange. The light is moved low to create the mood of dusk or sunset.

5.14 The same cityscape scene is now lit for nighttime with colored lights. A general light serves as an overall fill light, while a soft-blue light is the primary light source, perhaps simulating moonlight.

Using blue lights is very common and is a useful way to light your digital scenes for night. If you take a closer look at just about any evening shot in a traditional movie, you'll see a soft blue light used on the subject to separate it from the background. In addition, blue lights are often cast on buildings or objects to pull them out of the darkness, as in Figure 5.14.

Experiment with colored lights throughout your animations, as they can enhance, as well as guide, your viewer's mood and feeling. Colored lights can literally change the purpose of an image. Jeremy Birn's excellent book, *[digital] Lighting & Rendering* (New Riders Publishing, ISBN: 1-56205-954-8), has a tremendous amount of information on the technical aspects of lighting and color.

5.2 LIGHT AS A SUBJECT

You've read about the technical aspects of lighting, light temperature, and light color, but perhaps you've not considered light as a subject. Light can be used not just to illuminate your characters, sets, or objects, but also as a main focal point. For example: A shot calls for an eerie fog to rise over a dark, dank swamp. The sound of a rumbling ship fades up, and the viewer sees streaks of light through the mist. For this shot, instead of animating a complex UFO as the subject, light is used instead. This also helps make the scene more mysterious.

Light as a subject can be wide-ranging. The example of lights through the mist is only one way in which you can incorporate lights into your scenes. Because you're animating digitally, you can create characters solely out of light sources or use colored lights animated to music. Here are a few ideas for using lights as subjects:

- Volumetric, streaked lights for mysterious shots.

- Streaks of light through glass or windows to symbolize a higher being (see Figure 5.15).

- Streaks of light through a keyhole or crack in the floor to symbolize something creepy trying to escape (see Figure 5.16).

- Groups of lights shaped together, attached to a human bone structure, can create a soft, mystical figure (see Figure 5.17).

- A character in darkness holding a flashlight. The focus can be more on the action of the flashlight than the character, allowing the viewer to read a character's motions without actually seeing them.

Computer animation can be anything you make it. Lights in 3D applications are powerful and wide-ranging. Don't just think of them as tools to light your scene. Think of them as elements in your scene, just as you are thinking of the camera.

5.2.1 LIGHT POSITIONING

Lighting can be extremely complex, but there are some key things you can do to improve the lighting for just about any type of scene you might create. Light positioning is as important to digital cinematography and directing as is the position of the camera. Light, like camera shots, can make or break your scene. (See Figure 5.18.) So where would you begin? With so many different types of scenes, it's difficult to know how to set things up. You can begin with a few basic setups and move forward from there. Figure 5.19 shows a basic three-point lighting setup.

5.15 A simple room with light shining through a window can be the subject matter in many shots, as it can represent many different things.

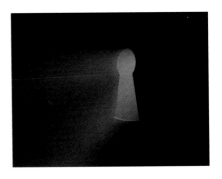

5.16 Streaks of light through a keyhole are a great way to generate viewer interest and develop mystery.

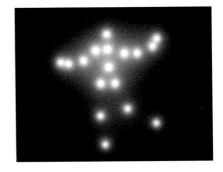

5.17 Lights can be directly positioned in the shape of characters for added creativity in your 3D scenes.

5.18 This is a bird's-eye view of the scene used to render Figure 5.13. To create the look of sunset, not only is the light color important, but its position is as well. Here you can see it's low and direct instead of high and general, as it would be in midday.

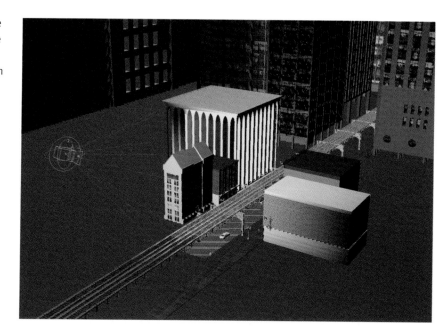

5.19 You can use basic three-point lighting as a starting ground for any studio-type scene. Product shots, dialogues, or even animated character auditions (a clever thing to do) can benefit from basic three-point lighting.

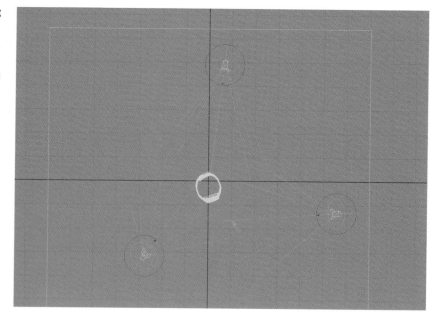

Three-point lighting involves a main light, called a *key light*, which is your primary light source. The key light usually is set to a soft white or amber color. Typically, it is placed about 40 degrees from the camera subject axis (point of origin) and is elevated between 30 and 45 degrees. The second light is called the *fill light* and usually is set close to opposite the key light. Tinted with color, such as a pale blue, the fill light's goal is to soften the shadows created by the key light. Its intensity or brightness is usually 40 percent or so less than the key light. The third light in a three-point lighting setup is the *back light*, also called the *hair light*. The back light separates the character or subject from the background. The color of this light is up to the gaffer (or animator) and can be anything. Often, a less bright, deep amber color works well. Figure 5.20 shows a render of Figure 5.19 using three-point lighting.

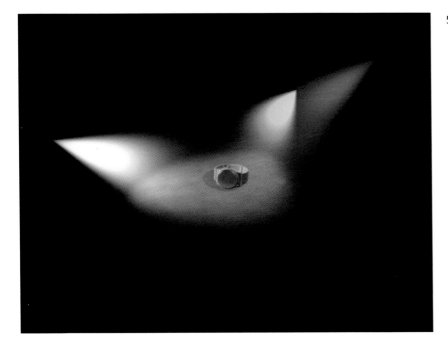

5.20 Three-point lighting, although basic, works well as a template for lighting studio-type scenes.

You can move beyond three-point lighting by applying the key, fill, and back lights in different arrangements for less traditional shots. Figure 5.21 shows a bedroom setup. In this shot, the time period is important. This shot is to be depicting a scene around the turn of the century. The main light source is the candle, as electricity hasn't been installed in this cabin just yet. The key light in this scene, then, is the candle. A fill light positioned high above the room acts as a fake bounce light. In the real world, the candlelight would bounce around the room to illuminate it. Instead of having your renderer calculate heavy-duty

5.21 Three-point lighting in this turn-of-the-century cabin works well when you position the key, fill, and back lights differently.

radiosity settings, you can use a fill light, colored like the candle, as a bounce light. A back light (or *kicker*) set to a soft blue and placed outside the window simulates moonlight and takes away blackness from the window area. This is a variation of three-point lighting with the lights arranged in different positions.

What about lighting an outdoor scene? In the real world, you begin with what available light you have. From there, you use reflectors to bounce light, and you add additional fill lights to soften shadows, brighten darker areas, and so on. In the computer environment, the available light is not an issue. You can create the necessary lights in your shots, often building them to resemble traditional lighting schemes. For example, the cityscape shot on the book's cover uses one large area light placed high in the sky to illuminate the street, buildings, and cars. The cover image has radiosity applied, allowing the objects' textures that are lit by the light source to be diffused throughout the image. Radiosity is a huge render hog, so in a frame-by-frame animation situation, you need a different setup. Figures 5.22 and 5.23 show two more lighting scenarios commonly used in film.

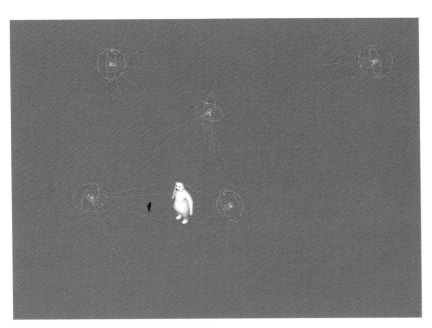

5.22 When working with characters as subjects, you can set up a lighting rig similar to the one shown here. Based on a three-point lighting setup, this rig adds more light to fill sets and backdrops.

5.23 If you're shooting a tight close-up on a subject, you can use a main soft area light and one fill light off camera to add distance to the shot and help establish an environment.

Lighting for computer graphics is unique within itself. It, like digital texturing or digital cinematography, is an art form all its own. Working through basic cinematic lighting principles while understanding the differences in light types, lighting environments, atmospheres, shadows, and the like is the smart way to set up your shots.

The next section describes the common types of lighting in computer animation packages and how you can use them.

5.3 COMPUTER-GENERATED LIGHTING

3D animation software has come a long way over the years. You know just by being in this field that it's often hard to decipher what's real and what's not in many of today's renders. There are really only a few variations in light types, but how and where those lights are placed, as well as what parameters are set, makes all the difference in your scenes.

The most common lights in 3D packages, *spotlights* are used for set lighting, scenery, effects, and more. They have many uses because they are controlled by both rotation and direction. *Distant lights* (also called directional lights) or *general lights* are best used for lighting larger areas, such as landscapes, cities, or oceans. Distant lights can be used as key or fill lights also, because they are defined by direction and can be controlled by rotation. Distant lights have no positional or distance requirements. For example, if you need to create that soft blue light in the background of a city street scene to illuminate buildings, you should use a distant light. *Omni* or *point lights* are useful for creating light bulbs, flares, or candles. Omni lights are controlled by position, not rotation. *Area lights* can give you the most natural simulation of local lighting, but they have a cost: render time. Area lights are controlled by direction and create soft, diffuse lighting. Figures 5.24 through 5.27 diagram spotlights, distant lights, omni lights, and area lights.

- Directional lights work only on rotation, and their position (or distance from a subject) does not matter.

- Rotational lights can be rotated to a specific direction, such as a spotlight.

- Positioned lights are lights whose distance is important. Point or omni lights are positioned lights. Although their position is important, rotation is not.

5.24 A single spotlight has both directional and rotational controls. The light source is deliberate and focused.

5.25 A single distant light has no directional value, only rotation. Notice how the back of the set is now lit, as well as the car.

5.26 A single point, or omni light, has no rotational value, but it's position (or direction) is important. Notice how the entire set is now lit.

5.27 A single area light's direction plays the most important role with this type of light. Also notice that it is a brighter light, with much softer shadows.

When used properly, any of these lights can produce excellent results for your production. Often, mixing light types can provide even better results, depending on your shot. For example, you have two characters that need to interact on a busy midday sidewalk. Use an area light to illuminate the entire scene, and place spotlights around the subjects to isolate them from the backdrop. A kicker light fills in any unnecessary shadows. A kicker is simply a nickname for a backlight, used to pull the subject from a background. Figure 5.28 shows the setup.

5.28 This scene incorporates mixed light types: one area light and three spotlights.

One of the cool things about lighting digitally is that the lights in your scene are not bound by cables or tripods. What's better, is that they can be animated. Animating lights can produce a completely unique look, such as:

- Animating a light that casts a shadow can produce unique and interesting effects. Further, an animated spotlight outside a window with Venetian blinds can produce the look of a car passing in the night.

- Tiny omni lights can be animated as bugs around a lantern. Omni lights animated like particles can be used to create sparks above a fire.

- Lights parented to wands or laser pointer objects can add that necessary glow at the end.

- Re-creating a concert stage could benefit from animated and colored spotlights.

Not only can a light's position and rotation be animated, so can the intensity falloff or dropoff, as well as a light's penumbra. The *penumbra* is partial shadowing from a light, specifically the area between complete shadow and complete illumination. The brightness of light changing over time is useful for instantly identifying a subject. Or perhaps a character flips a switch as he walks into a room, turning on a light. Bursts of energy or fire can be created with animated light intensities. You can go a step further and animate light colors as well. Perhaps your concert stage needs a cycling color disco dance light. Well, maybe a colored spotlight at least!

5.3.1 LIGHT FALLOFF

Lighting in the traditional world naturally dissipates. The headlights on a car illuminate only a small area. The candlestick on the nightstand brightens only so much. In the computer, however, you need to define the property. Simply put, *falloff* is the decrease of illumination intensity the farther the subject is from the light. Falloff intensity is inversely proportional to the square of distance. In other words, if you move an object twice as far from a light source, the object receives one-quarter as much light. Most applications have a range of falloff settings. Figure 5.29 shows the falloff options available for LightWave 3D. You can see quite a few falloff values based on inverse square distance.

Using falloff on lights is helpful when trying to specifically light a scene. Say you have two characters driving a car with the camera facing them from the hood. The interior of the car is lit just right, the outside lighting is properly set, but the characters are too dark. Adding another spotlight will brighten them, but you run the risk of lighting more of the car's interior. Using the right falloff setting, you can constrain the light to just the distance and area you desire. To determine the right falloff settings, use your object and scene size ratios to determine the distance of the subject from the light.

5.29 Programs such as LightWave 3D have many settings for light intensity falloff.

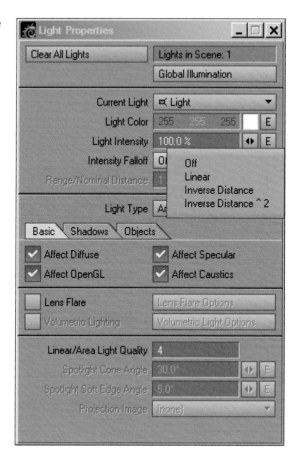

5.3.2 LIGHTING FOR MOODS

You've probably done it yourself at some point in your life. You know, dim the lights and set the mood? Lighting in the computer gives you the control to create any situation you can imagine. By using the right combination of intensity and color, you can effectively create a mood for your cinematic masterpiece. Don't confuse mood with comfort, however. The mood at home is usually more calm, warm, and relaxed than an office lit with cold, greenish fluorescent lights. Granted, there are many other factors involved with different moods, but lighting is a key ingredient.

What can you do to create different moods with lighting for your production? You can start by identifying the mood you want to create. Do you want a stark and cold environment? If so, light it with very pale grayish-blue lights and harsh shadows. Avoid fill lights, as these will soften the hard shadows and, hence, soften the mood. Perhaps you want to create a warm, soothing, and dreamlike mood. Maybe your character is having flashbacks to the crush he had on his teacher. Change the lighting to a light warm brown and boost the intensity so the viewer understands it's a dream. Lighting can play a key role in identifying the changing of shots too, such as switching from the here and now to a dream, a memory, or a future premonition.

Mood lighting is really nothing more than changing the color, intensity, and sometimes position of your light sources. Picture how you want the mood to be, and set your variables accordingly by using a combination of these settings.

5.3.3 SHADOWS

Shadows, like many elements in 3D animation, can be controlled unlike in the traditional filmmaking world. This is sometimes bad, but often good. It's bad because you need to apply specific settings and, of course, use more render time to get true-to-life shadows. These shadows are usually generated from an area light. Controlled shadows are good because they are just that—controlled. You can set how soft you want a shadow, its color, or its opacity.

Shadows can be controlled in many ways and can be extremely important to the overall look of your project. Using shadows helps define placement of characters and helps identify depth. Figure 5.30 shows a simple object lit with an area light. The shadows cast help give the object depth and height, while increasing its realism.

5.30 Even simple objects gain a sense of space, depth, and realism when shadows are created with an area light.

Shadows can be a creative tool in your projects, more than just a result of light. Perhaps you've done some architectural modeling and walk-through renderings. During your animation, you need to show the outside of the building, which is surrounded by large maple trees. Instead of modeling and rendering every tree, you need to see only the effects of the shadows in the close-up you plan. By using a black-and-white image, called a *cookie* or *gobo*, you can project shadows from a single light source to make it look as if the light was casting shadows through the trees. Figure 5.31 shows the image used to project a shadow from a spotlight, and Figure 5.32 shows the result.

5.31 A high contrast photograph of a tree and its leaves can be used in your digital creations as a gobo or "cookie."

5.32 Once the gobo is applied to a light source, the light is cast "through" the gobo, simulating shadows through branches of tree.

Shadows can also be colored, allowing you to create a different look altogether. Figure 5.33 shows a simple object with a standard dark shadow, while Figure 5.34 shows the same object with three colored lights, each casting a colored shadow.

5.33 A pretty standard shadow.

5.34 A much more elaborate set of shadows.

Experiment with using colored shadows in your application, as well as using shadowing as a tool. If you've ever worked in video or film, you know that shadows can be a nightmare in some situations. Luckily, in the computer environment you have full control and can even decide not to include shadows at all.

5.4 LIGHT AS A TOOL

In 3D applications, the camera and lights are two of your most important tools. Think of lighting for digital cinematography and directing as a tool. It's a tool than enables you not only to illuminate your scenes and subjects, but also to create moods, feelings, and special effects. Light is everything, and it's one of the key ingredients in your 3D animations. The other key ingredient is the camera, and how you direct it goes hand in hand with how you create your lights.

Read on to Chapter 6, "[digital] Directing," to learn about setting up subjects, framing, types of shots, and more.

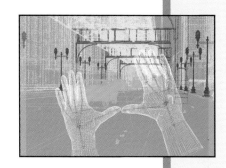

6

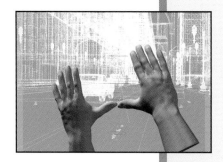

[DIGITAL] DIRECTING

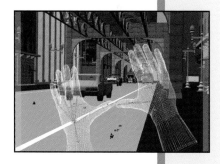

D IGITAL DIRECTING IS NOT something most 3D animators aspire to when learning their craft. It involves vision, planning, and a knowledge of key cinematic principles. This chapter will help you develop your directing skills by first taking a look at situations that traditional directors deal with on each project. This chapter will focus on shot flow, working with subjects, and the types of shots you can use in your animations. In addition, it will instruct you on directing the camera in 3D space.

Traditional directorial experience is always a bonus when you sit down in front of the computer to direct a 3D animation. Of course, not everyone has a directing background, and on some levels, that can be a good thing. Whatever your situation, this chapter will guide you through the directorial process as it applies to computer generated storytelling. You might think that you're not a director—you're an animator, right? What happens when you close your eyes and think about your animation short? What do you envision, and how do you see your shots? Believe it or not, this is your first step in directing! Directing is the interpretation of a story.

6.1 THINKING LIKE A DIRECTOR

Part of visualizing your entire production is to also visualize your shots. Directing for film, video, or animation takes the ability to see things before they happen, and consequently, makes them happen. It's your job to bring the vision to life or, at least, to render! Visualization is really nothing more than bringing your ideas and thoughts to life.

Your goal as a director is to convey a story through images and sound. Chapter 3, "Storyboards," discussed the visualization process through drawn images. This process is essential to directing, as it provides a framework and blueprint for the production at hand. Storyboarding, like any plan, can change, and you should be open to new ideas. This means that, as a director, you should be open to the fact that ideas, shots, and situations may change during the production process. Visualizing your 3D animation is planning; directing is action. Beyond this, your drive and goal are means to an end, and your job is to make every shot work.

As a digital content creator, you have one great advantage. People don't just watch a movie, they throw themselves into it. Often critical and untrusting, even impatient, the moviegoer wants to be lost in what he or she is viewing. You have the ability to make this happen. Your job as a digital cinematographer and director is to ensure that the audience does not lose interest.

Your first and best weapon against viewer boredom is the story. The story's cinematic fuel feeds the actors' emotions and dialogue, and it helps the director decide what camera shots to use. The story, and how the film or animation unfolds, should make viewers examine themselves or the world around them. The cinematic fuel of any story is the cinematography and the dialogue. For example, the cover project of this book takes place on an interesting city street. Your awareness is piqued, and you want to know more. As the director introduces characters, the story unfolds. The viewer is curious, intrigued, and wants to see what happens next. The perfect blend of shots, dialogue, and story keep the ball rolling.

Of course, the film and animation direction process can be more complicated, and this chapter can't be a substitute for intensive study of the subject or years of filmmaking experience. What it can be, however, is a guide to help you work through your shots—how to visualize them, set them up, and deal with their content.

6.1.1 SHOT FLOW

What is shot flow? It begins with planning, like anything else. It is about continuity and the overall movement of your production. Shot flow begins by understanding what each shot conveys to the viewer and how each shot transitions to the next. A sequence of shots carries the viewer from one point to another, in a logical progression, and it is a director's job to see this through. Although a shot can be constructed of many elements, it needs two basic ingredients:

- Camera angle
- Frame size

The right camera angle, in combination with frame size, produces an image that is not only balanced, but also flows. Viewers must feel that what they watch makes sense. To the viewer, a change in camera angles, a variation in a shadow, or a change in a character's position can break the flow of a shot. When these, or any other elements are out of place between shots, viewers can become disoriented and confused, and they can lose interest.

Shot flow is important for both the director and the cinematographer in that what they create together is what the editor works with. The cinematographer and director create a space within which the editor works. In Chapter 11, "Editing," you'll see how the editing process, although it occurs at the end of the production cycle, is something to be considered throughout pre-production, planning, and shooting. Editing is an integral part of making shots "flow," and to begin making a shot flow, the director must first understand how subjects, be they characters, sets, props, or inanimate objects, should be framed.

6.1.2 COMPOSITION

Directing animation varies from job to job. If you are the director of a two-hour animated feature, your job involves instructing the animators, whose job it is to animate the characters to the dialogue that a scriptwriter has written. It's also your job to direct the technical animators who are lighting the digital production. On a smaller scale, you may be someone who is not only the director, but also the cinematographer and animator all in one. This chapter assumes you're doing all three jobs, and it begins with framing.

The subjects you set up in your animations can be anything your digital camera views. They can be inanimate objects, light sources, scenery, the camera itself, or perhaps digital people. For the examples here, the cover shot of this book will be the set and digital people will be the actors. Determining how a shot should be set up and where subjects should be placed depends on:

- The story, dialogue, or scene at hand
- The current lighting situation
- How the set and surroundings affect the shot
- Keeping the flow of the scene
- What you have envisioned for the shot

A story is what drives a film. It is what fuels the animated short. Even if there's no dialogue, there is always a reason or goal to an animation. The director interprets this goal and determines the most appropriate shot. To set up a shot, you must first ask yourself some questions. What is the purpose of this shot? How does it flow with the shots that come before and after it? And how does this shot represent what the story (and the director's vision) is trying to say?

The following examples can help you identify some general directing situations. As a start, Figure 6.1 shows a shot where two people meet on the street and begin a casual dialogue.

6.1 A casual dialogue between two people can be directed with a comfortable shot from third person point of view.

Now the dialogue between the two people becomes heated and con-frontational. The shot should change to fit the dialogue. The camera moves close, and the shot gets tight as the digital actors get into it. Confrontation between the actors is uncomfortable, and the shot should represent it as such. Figure 6.2 shows the shot.

6.2 As the dialogue between the actors becomes heated, the shot becomes tight and slightly uncomfortable.

As the heated dialogue between the two continues, the director wants viewers to feel the anger of one digital actor. To do this, the camera now changes from a third person point of view to a first person point of view—the second digital actor's point of view. You are now the recipient of the anger, as shown in Figure 6.3.

As you can see, directing in the computer involves significant camera work. Remember, the types of shots you set up and the shots you direct are what your viewer not only will see, but will feel as well.

6.3 To convey one digital actor's anger, the shot is now placed in first person. You, as the viewer, have the anger directed at you.

6.2 TYPES OF SHOTS

Knowing how to direct your animation means knowing what type of shots to use. Shots in your scene can be used to change a point of view, reveal story information, or establish a mood. Figure 6.4 diagrams *framing heights* from bottom to top for a camera. Figure 6.5 shows additional framing heights. In other words, it shows the common and most-used shot descriptions and their appropriate size based on an average person.

As directors discuss and plan shots for an animation, they often describe the shots as "cut to a close-up" or "pan to a full shot." And while these are terms used more during the editing process (see Chapter 11, "Editing"), they are important to the director as well. While a director must concentrate on so many individual aspects of a production, he or she must also think about how the editing process will bring those individual elements together. The diagrams in Figure 6.4 identify approximately how tight the camera should be on each different shot. Not all shots need to be used, and they can vary depending on the situation. A few of the key shots you'll use often are close-up shots, medium shots, and full shots.

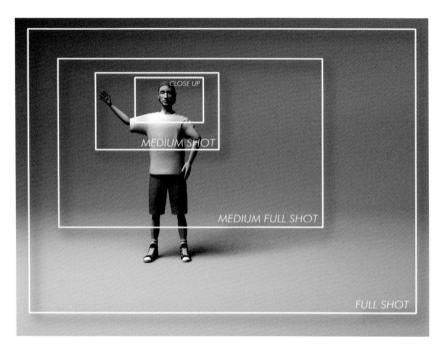

6.4 These common framing heights are based on an average person.

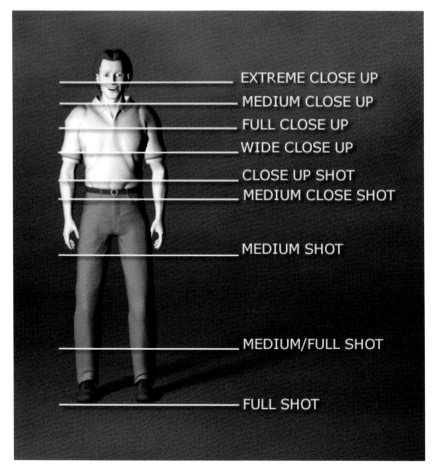

6.5 Additional framing options based on an average person.

6.2.1 CLOSE-UP SHOTS

Close-up shots are dramatic and intimate. You can use a *close-up shot* for dialogue, also referred to as a "talking head." In the digital environment, using a close-up shot on a dialogue sequence serves more than one purpose. First, it brings the viewer into the action. Second, it saves you, or your staff, time and effort because the shot is full with a single subject. For example, Figure 6.6 shows a close-up shot of a character. The shot only needs a small amount of backdrop visible. This means that less geometry, less lighting, and less motion need to be performed. This also means that there will be less rendering.

Of course, your entire animation can't be comprised of close-up shots, but when organized and planned appropriately, close-ups not only help tell the story, but save time. The close-up shot also allows the viewer to see the emotion of the character, which is important to telling the story. The close-up shot can vary, depending on the composition. Later in Chapter 8, "Lines of Action," you'll learn how you can use a close-up shot in various ways, along with the other types of shots described here.

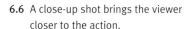

6.6 A close-up shot brings the viewer closer to the action.

MEDIUM SHOTS

The *medium shot* is a general, all-purpose shot. Medium shots are used for dialogue sequences, and they allow the viewer to pick up on the character's movements and gestures. Body language is important to conveying emotion, and the medium shot remains close enough to capture that emotion. Medium shots are also good for small group shots, such as a conversation between characters. The medium shot often is partnered with a close-up shot, because it is not necessarily used for establishing shots. (Shots that establish a group's composition will be discussed in Chapter 7, "Staging.") Medium shots are best for individuals or small groups; more than three or four people in the scene will require you to use a different type of shot. Figure 6.7 shows a typical medium shot.

Although medium shots are good for dialogue shots—allowing the viewer to still be a part of a character's emotion—a full shot is often needed. Full shots are beneficial to show body language, nervousness, and even anticipation. Perhaps the character in the city street is very uncomfortable with his new mob friends. A medium shot could bring the viewer closer to the actor's face, perhaps to see a furrowed brow or a bead of sweat. A full shot on the actor can show a tapping foot and awkward hand movements, emphasizing the nervousness.

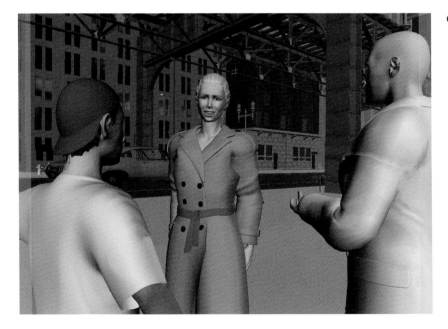

6.7 Medium shots are good for dialogues and small gatherings.

6.2.3 WIDE AND FULL SHOTS

Wide and *full* shots are the launching pads for many scenes a director will put together. They help establish a character in a specific location. For example, a boy walks out of doorway onto an empty street. A close-up or medium shot would not allow viewers to see where the character is. The wide shot helps identify both the character and his environment. These shots also allow characters to show body language. Although emotion is important in a close-up and medium shot, body language is important in a full shot as well. Figure 6.8 shows a wide shot of a boy in a cityscape. The goal of the shot is to establish the single character's position in the frame and his relationship to his surroundings. The director can slowly zoom the camera in to a full, then medium shot to bring the viewer's attention to the boy's dialogue or emotion. When that happens, the audience already will understand where the boy is because of the wide establishing shot.

6.8 A full shot establishes and connects a character with his environment.

Shots you choose to use as a digital director can be changed quite easily, unlike a traditional filmmaker. A traditional filmmaker needs to worry about many elements in a scene if a shot needs to be changed. The actors need to redo their parts, lighting and props need to be adjusted, and background elements such as cars and people need to be reset. For the digital filmmaker, it's a only a matter of changing the camera! Although traditional filmmaking principles, such as close-up and full shots still apply, how you use them within a scene is much easier. The following is a formal list of shots you can refer to when planning, storyboarding, or directing animation:

- Extreme close-up

- Close-up

- Medium close-up

- Medium shot

- Full (figure)

- Medium wide

- Wide

- Extreme wide (or distant)

> **NOTE**
>
> The shot list here refers to both sets and characters. The first five are for characters, while the last three are primarily for sets or establishing shots.

6.2.4 CUT-AWAY SHOTS

Close-ups, medium shots, and full shots not only have a purpose individually, but as a whole. For example, a full shot can establish the location of a dialogue shot, then the director can "cut away" to a medium shot to identify the recipient and avoid an awkward cut. A formal "cut-away" shot cuts away from the action at hand to something else. For example, the boy in the cityscape meets up with his Mafia friends. They have a dialogue, and during that dialogue, an eyewitness looking out a nearby window sees the conversation. The director can cut away to the eyewitness both to introduce a new element in the story and enable the dialogue shot to change in some way, such as camera angle. Transitioning from a full shot to another full shot is uncomfortable for the viewer, and it breaks the shot flow. The *cut-away shot* allows the director to transition between similar shots, such as a full shot to a full shot, by cutting to a different type of shot, such as a medium shot, in between. A cut-away shot can be used to merge similar shots together or to hide mistakes. Figures 6.9 and 6.10 show two shots: one a is dialogue, and the other is a cut-away from the eyewitness point of view. Here, the cut-away shot helps break the monotony of the dialogue shot while enabling the viewer to gain a sense of to whom the character is speaking.

6.9 A dialogue shot between two characters. It's a lengthy conversation, so a cut-away shot can help break up the monotony.

6.10 A cut-away shot breaks up what could be a long dialogue, and it also introduces the viewer to a secret eyewitness peering from a building window.

Cut-always are just one way for a director to change a shot. While close-
ups, medium shots, and full shots are generally used with a static camera,
you can animate the camera for a different look.

6.2.5 DOLLY SHOTS

One of the greatest things about 3D animation is that your only limitation is your imagination. You are not limited by cables, talent, unions,
natural lighting conditions, or other factors. As a digital director, you
have control over everything in your scene, enough to make a traditional
director jealous! Because you're not limited, you are often able to do
things in the digital filmmaking world that are not always possible in
the traditional.

A *dolly shot* is a very natural shot where the camera moves horizontally
across a scene. For example, stand up and take a look at something across
the room. Now walk, but stay focused on that item; this is how a dolly
shot looks. The dolly shot allows a director to follow action in a scene,
such as a dog walking down the street looking for the next bright red
fire hydrant. In the traditional world, a director employs either a hand-
held camera, a steadycam, or a dolly on a track. Digitally, you can make
a smooth motion with just two keyframes or add a hand-held camera
look. Again, digital content creators have more control than traditional
directors. Figure 6.11 shows an example of a dolly shot, from its starting
point to the ending point.

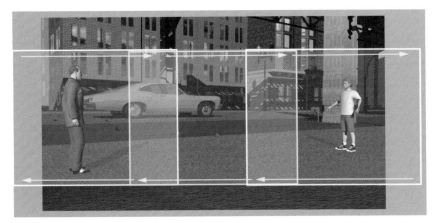

6.11 A dolly shot moves the camera across
the horizontal axis, following the
action or revealing a character
or prop.

There are several types of dolly shots:

- Character dolly

- Pull-back reveal

- Depth dolly

- Expand dolly

- Contract dolly

Directors often use a *character dolly* to focus on one or more characters in a scene. This shot is also commonly known as a *push-in*. The camera starts out with a full, or even medium shot, and is pushed in forward. You can push the camera all the way up to an extreme close-up if needed. Push-ins add tension to a scene and magnify a character's emotion. Faster motions can be used for a more comic approach.

The *pull-back reveal* is used to reveal the full extent of a scene. For example, the camera is focused up close on a lost little boy looking for his mother. As he becomes scared and increasingly worried, the shot pulls back to reveal the boy standing alone in the middle of a large crowd. The viewers gain a sense of the enormity of the boy's situation.

A *depth dolly* can be used when characters move toward and away from the camera. The camera moves past characters or objects that temporarily block the field of view, helping to emphasize the depth of a scene.

In an *expand dolly shot*, the camera follows a character who is moving away. As the camera moves forward, the actor walks away faster than the camera. The viewer feels distanced from the character with a shot like this. You might use an expand dolly to end a scene. Additionally, you can reverse this type of shot to introduce a character to a scene.

A *contract dolly* moves the camera forward as a character walks or moves toward the camera at the same time. This type of shot makes a simple action more dramatic by combining two opposite actions. A variation of this could have the character move toward the camera while the camera pans up, revealing the subject.

6.2.6 PANS

The dolly shot moves along with the action in a scene, but the *pan shot* follows the action from a fixed position—the camera moves rotationally on the horizontal axis. Turn your head from left to right, and you've just seen what a pan shot looks like. Camera pans are great for establishing shots, either with a full shot or close-up. This use of a pan is sometimes called *reframing a shot*. Simply put, reframing a shot can be thought of as a "slight pan." For example, two characters on the street are having a dialogue, then a cut-away shot to above the characters from an eyewitness standpoint introduces a new character. When the shot cuts away, a slight pan can be used to reframe the shot so that the eyewitness's face enters the frame. Directors typically use pan shots to view a panorama, such as a landscape or large room, that does not fit into a single static shot. It's a great way to follow characters as they move. Figure 6.12 shows a large scene with two shots representing the starting and ending points of a pan shot.

6.12 A long street viewed from an angle has a fixed camera that moves from left to right. This example shows the beginning and ending frames of a pan shot.

6.2.7 TILTS

A *tilt* follows the action vertically, like an up-and-down pan. Tilts are great for following the action of a rocket blasting off or for emphasizing the tall expanse of a skyscraper. Figure 6.13 shows the starting and ending of shots of a tilt.

6.13 Similar to a pan, the tilt rotates the camera on the vertical axis from a fixed position. This is a great way to follow the action of any vertically moving subject or to simply view the expanse of a tall building.

6.2.8 ZOOMS

Zoom shots involve motion of the focal length; the camera itself does not translate. Although many animators overlook this technique, the zoom is a great shot to use in 3D animation. For example, if you pick up just a simple camcorder, you often zoom in to get a closer look at the action. Why not in 3D? You can use zooms for fast-moving action, surprises, explosions, or anything that you can think of. A zoom can bring your shot from a full shot to a close-up without movement of the camera—a zoom has a distinctly different look from a dolly. It can be used in just about any type of animation, from logo design to character animation to legal animation. Figures 6.14 and 6.15 show a scene with first a full shot, then a zoom.

6.14 A low-angle shot looking down the city street allows the viewer to focus on the scene.

6.15 Zooming in on the '57 Chevy brings the viewer closer to the action.

Zoom shots can be done slowly and easily to to bring the viewer into a scene or character. Zoom shots can also be done quickly as an added effect to your animations. Say, for example, your animated character's expression needs to change quickly from calm to surprised. A quick zoom into his face helps emphasize the surprise. Zooms can be fast or slow, in or out. They are also great when mixed with a shaking camera to simulate a hand-held camcorder look.

> **NOTE**
>
> Whether you use a zoom or a dolly shot is simply a matter of preference. The difference is that zooming changes the perspective as it changes the focal length. (See Chapter 2, "The [digital] Camera" for more on focal length.) If you don't want the perspective to change in the shot, you can just use a dolly shot and move the camera in (or out). Remember, in 3D you can move the camera freely— no wires, no cables, no operators!

6.2.9   BOOM AND CRANE SHOTS

Using mechanical shots is one of the more exciting areas of shooting digitally, because while such shots can be difficult to accomplish in the physical world, you do not have the same limitations when working digitally. *Mechanical shots* are often referred to as boom or crane shots. These techniques traditionally use cranes or jibs, which are "arms" that move the camera into difficult-to-access places. For example, have you ever seen an opening shot to a scene that starts high up in the trees and moves down slowly to focus in on the action? A crane shot like this is expensive and often difficult to set up for film or video, but comes without hassle for the computer animator. Mechanical shots help the director create interesting camera moves and view the action through unique angles. Figures 6.16 and 6.17 show the starting and ending frames of a mechanical shot. The camera starts high over the street above the elevated tracks and moves down across the street as a car passes underneath. It would be a very difficult shot to film in the real world, but in the computer, you're not limited by a mechanical crane, cables, or traffic!

In 3D animation, it's easy to create a full scene and create your shots within it, such as the cityscape used for many of the examples in this chapter. A full scene allows the director to frame out full shots, medium shots, or close-ups without having to re-create sets or props. In traditional drawn or hand animation, this technique is called a *field cut*, and it enables the animator to gain as many shots as possible from one drawn frame. You can employ this technique in 3D, as well.

6.16 The beginning frame of a crane shot. It can start high (or low) as the camera begins to move.

6.17 The ending frame of a crane shot. The camera has moved down from above the tracks and seamlessly traveled between the rails. Try that in the real world!

6.2.10 PULL-FOCUS SHOTS

A pull- (or rack-) focus shot is more natural than you might think, so it's surprising that the shot is not used more in 3D animation. If you're standing on a street corner having a conversation with two other people, your eye cannot focus on all that is happening around your field of vision. Your eye can either focus on something close-up or far away. To look from one to the other, your eye refocuses; this is exactly what the camera does in a *pull-focus shot*.

Camera lenses can't focus on everything in a scene at once, and their focus needs to change to follow the action. In the computer environment, everything is always in focus. This is a good thing for the novice, as it is one less thing to worry about. For the professional, this is yet another element you need to be aware of and take action upon. One of the subtle differences between professional and amateur animations is the use of pull-focus shots and depth of field—making the computer's eye work like a human eye. Although full shots and close-ups are more commonplace, mechanical and pull-focus shots allow you to take the viewer to a new perspective. As a digital director, you need to be aware of this and use pull-focus shots when appropriate. Figures 6.18 and 6.19 show the start and end of a pull-focus shot.

6.18 In this shot, the camera is fixed but focused on the character in the backdrop. Your eye is drawn to that character.

6.19 When the pull-focus is applied, a shift in the view brings your attention to the character in the foreground.

6.2.11 SHOT ABBREVIATIONS

When planning animations, the director works through scripts and storyboards. As shot planning progresses, film and video directors often use abbreviations for the shots they need. When putting together your 3D animation's shot flow, you can use the same standard abbreviations:

- **POV**   Point of view
- **OTS**   Over the shoulder
- **FG**   Foreground
- **BG**   Background
- **ELS**   Extreme long shot
- **LS**   Long shot
- **FS**   Full shot
- **MS**   Medium shot
- **CU**   Close-up
- **MCU**   Medium close-up
- **ECU**   Extreme close-up

Even when creating simple notes about your animation, shot abbreviations are useful for planning your shots.

6.3 THE NEXT STEP

Feature film, video, and animation production schedules are virtually the same through scheduling, shot planning, storyboarding, and creative direction. Whether traditionally or digitally, the director is responsible for the vision of the film and the visual decisions that determine shot flow and camera placement. Although a production designer in the traditional world is responsible for set design, costumes, and props, the digital director often is responsible for these as well.

Digital directing is more than instructing people on how you'd like things accomplished in your production, and it's more than positioning actors, lights, and cameras. Learning to be a digital director means understanding the tools to bring a vision to life. You need to be an interpreter, an inventor, and a manager. Although much of your work involves modeling, texturing, lighting, animation, and rendering, keep in mind some of the issues a director faces in the traditional world.

One of a digital director's primary functions is shot planning and shot flow—making sure that the overall animation process remains a focused goal. Another key aspect a director needs to consider is staging. Read on to Chapter 7, "Staging," to learn how this key ingredient can enhance your digital masterpiece.

NOTE

Be sure to check out the *American Cinematographer Film Manual.* It is an indispensible resource for all things related to camera and film. Visit **www.studiodepot.com/asc/**.

7

STAGING

S TAGING IS THE POSITIONING of digital actors, props, their environment, and where they exist in relation to the camera. It is spatial design that highlights the important visual or emotional material within a scene. Staging is as important to setting up your shots as the shot itself is. Staging and composition go hand in hand. This chapter will explore the importance of the following concepts:

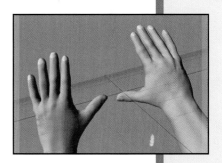

- Character staging and blocking
- Balanced poses
- Staging dialogue sequences
- Staging action scenes
- Staging dramatic scenes
- The rule of thirds

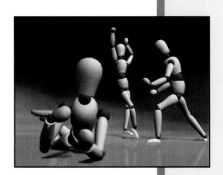

The chapter also briefly discusses various methods you can use to direct your digital actors. From balance to symmetry, a character's body language and how it moves through the scene is important to properly staging your shots. There are few directors who have mastered the art of staging—the placement of characters in just the right place at just the right time. Digitally, it is something you can master with practice, often much faster than a traditional and seasoned director. Why? Because you have more control over your digital character's motion. A traditional director is dealing with many uncontrollable elements, such as sunlight or natural sound. But in the computer, you are the one who is making the actors move. You are the one who changes the lighting and adds the sound. You are also the one who places the camera.

Camera location is as important to staging as character position. You need to consider what and how the digital camera sees. This chapter will guide you through placing your camera, but it will begin with staging characters for animation individually. From there, you'll see how you can place multiple characters, and eventually set up a complete shot.

7.1 CHARACTER STAGING

Knowing just how to position the characters in your scene is the first step in knowing how to shoot them. Like traditional film, theater, or painting, animation is an art form that you are always working to perfect. So where should you begin? You've planned your animations, worked out the storyboards, and decided on shots. The next logical step is placing your digital actors in their environments.

You want characters to appear natural, not forced, while still being able to deliver their dialogues and body language. Body language is important, and viewers will pick up on it right away. Viewers also pick up on a lack of it; an unnaturally posed character is often more noticeable than you might think. A good pose with body language is always properly balanced. Proper balance comes from good weight and proper shadows.

Weighting your characters is a little more work than you might realize. It's very tempting to pose a character the way you think. Instead, you should pose a character to the way you *move*. The best way to achieve good, balanced characters is to get up, get to a mirror, and stand there. Watch how your body moves. Going one better, set a video camera on a tripod and tape yourself posing. Walk into the frame and turn to face the camera. Rest on one leg, then transfer your weight to another. You'll see that your body, when relaxed, uses the strength of your leg to support you. (See Figure 7.1.)

NOTE

If you want to explore beyond the basic techniques presented here, George Maestri's excellent *[digital] Character Animation* series (New Riders Publishing) is the key resource for understanding and applying poses, weight, and motion to your characters.

7.1 A standing figure is balanced appropriately, resting her weight on one leg. Balanced poses give the character proper weight and placement.

Natural-looking characters need to be asymmetrical. That is, just because one side of the body does something does not mean that the other side should do the same. It's very easy for animators to move both sides in exactly the same way, but in reality the human form does not work like that. If a character is walking, how do you position the character so that the viewer knows if the walk is merely a casual walk or a hurried walk to the bathroom? Let's say that a crazy mob boss is after you. You're on an empty city street, and there's no where to hide. How would you move? Would your character just run, or would the character move like there's no tomorrow? How would you animate the difference? The run would not be steady and even. It would be fast and awkward because the character is rushing. In addition, the character's weight should be shifted forward. In Figure 7.2, the weight of the character is moved forward, with arms and legs in long strides. The weight shifted forward tells the viewer right away that this guy is in a hurry.

7.2 A character's weight is pulled toward his front to emphasize an urgency in his walk.

Effectively staging your characters means you must give them not only balance and weight, but also proper positioning within the scene. If a camera shot shows a character on the edge of a building, you, as the viewer, will not get a sense of his fear or the severity of the situation unless the camera is staged properly as well. Figure 7.3 shows a character near the edge of a high building. The poor staging of the camera allows you to see that the character is up high, but there is no emphasis on just how high he is. Figure 7.4 shows the same scene, but with the camera changed to a wide angle and tilted down to show the severity of the character's situation. Will he fall? Will he jump?

Understanding how to stage your camera properly means understanding types of shots, available lenses, and lines of action. Chapter 8, "Lines of Action," discusses camera angles and continuity. Those elements, combined with the proper staging of your characters and subjects, will help bring your directorial vision to the viewer.

For now, however, read on and take a look at some general staging situations and some methods you can use to stage your characters in almost any situation.

NOTE

It's important always to study movies and television. Pay close attention to how characters and cameras are placed through the various shots, and mimic these setups in your 3D work.

7.3 The staging of the camera in this shot is poorly done. It does not convey a sense of urgency for the character's situation.

7.4 Although the character remains in the same position, the staging of the camera in this shot shows the danger the character is facing.

7.1.1 DIALOGUE SEQUENCE STAGING

Staging for dialogue requires you to focus on two things: the characters' emotions and relationships between the characters. Based on these, you can determine the position of the camera. In the traditional world, balancing character relationships and camera position can be quite a challenge. In the digital world, it is much easier. Remember, you are the one making the characters move, talk, and interact. You are not limited by the attitudes of the talent or the cables of the camera. You are free to create your own vision as you see it, without interference.

To begin staging for your characters, you first must consider what they are saying. Think about how a person positions him- or herself during a particular dialogue. If it's a casual conversation, how are they standing? Perhaps the dialogue is heated, so how would the characters interact? Figures 7.5 through 7.8 explore different dialogues and the possible staging you could set up for 3D characters.

7.5 Conversational dialogue sequences should have your characters staged comfortably. The spacing between them is modest, and their body language is relaxed.

7.6 Confrontational dialogue sequences should have your characters closer together. The space between them is close and uncomfortable. Their body language is tense.

7.7 Emotional dialogue sequences can have your characters physically interacting.

7.8 Emotional dialogue sequences can have your characters standing apart from each other, similar to the staging often seen in soap operas. This is often called a television two-shot.

Emotional scenes, as well as physical or confrontational ones, can be staged in a variety of ways. The example figures show basic setups that you can work with, but of course your story and dialogue are going to drive the positions of your characters and camera. To better understand the issues involved, however, take a closer look at the emotional staging pictured in Figure 7.8.

The characters are not facing each other. In an emotional scene, body language is very important. Having a character turn her back on another increases the emotion to the viewer. Even without words, you pick up on the sensitivity and tense situation at hand. Another benefit of staging your emotional characters like this is that the viewer can see both actors' faces and reactions at the same time. Perhaps the character in the foreground is hiding a deep dark secret, but can't stand to face the other character. Facing the viewer with her back to the opposite character allows the viewer to pick up on facial expressions that can signify a lie, fear, or sadness.

When dealing with confrontational situations, the staging can work similarly to that of emotional scenes. Characters can physically interact, or they can be standing apart. One actor can have his back turned to the other just like the emotional shot, but this time out of rage and disgust. Again, the facial expressions of both characters can be seen when you stage the scene like this.

7.1.2 ACTION SEQUENCE STAGING

Staging for action sequences is almost more important for the cinematographer than it is for the director. This is because action involves motion and timing. But while the camera needs to be staged appropriately, the director still needs to consider where and how the actors are positioned. To stage a character for an action sequence properly, you need to assess the scene properly. One way to prepare yourself is to define the starting and ending positions of the action sequence. Figures 7.9 and 7.10 show the start and end of an action sequence.

7.9 Staging for action sequences is more difficult than for dialogue sequences because action means motion. To help set up the shot, you can stage the character's starting position. In this shot, the character is ready to take a leap from a tall building.

7.10 Staging for action sequences will often rely more on the motion of the camera. Placement of your character's ending frame, however, will help set the full staging for the scene.

Action sequence staging will rely heavily on the interaction between the characters and the camera, as well as the environment in the scene. As you read through the rest of this chapter, take note of the various staging methods to help position your characters for any type of shot you might need. Chapter 8, "Lines of Action," will help you plan out the necessary camera angles as well.

Staging for action shots can be more than just a desperate boy jumping off of a building. Perhaps the scene calls for an explosion, and a character gets thrown toward the camera. How do you go about staging this? The following is a checklist that you can use when planning action staging. Prior to shooting a scene, make mental notes of the important points that the shot needs. For example:

- The boy needs to look afraid in the beginning of the shot.
- The mob boss enters the frame, pointing a gun.
- The explosion suddenly goes off, saving the boy from being shot.

Make sure you can get all of these points across in the shot. Be sure that you know where you are coming from before this shot and where you are going after it. This is a sort of mental editing—putting shots together in your head so that when you create each individual one, they flow together seamlessly.

7.2   GENERAL SCENE STAGING

A dramatic scene can incorporate emotional dialogue and action. As a director, you need to train your eye to see all possible situations of setup and character placement. This book started with talk about visualization, and staging your characters relies on that vision. Dramatic scenes, as well as action or dialogue sequences, can benefit from some general staging practices. Dramatic scenes involve key staging of your characters. Whether there is dialogue or not, the positioning and interaction of the actors is what drives the scene more than any camera placement and movement. Remember that there is not necessarily a right or a wrong way to stage any scene, but there are some standards you can use. The information here can help you make the best decision when positioning characters.

Traditional techniques in filmmaking work very well in the computer, but often your own interpretation and plain old common sense can help you position characters and set up your shots. Don't be locked to one simple plan. Have a plan, but know that variations are always a possibility. After all, you're working digitally, and changes are as easy as they are possible. To help you get comfortable making these decisions, review Figure 7.11, which shows a diagram that you can use for one or two character staging. This image can give you an idea of how to map out and plan character placement with camera positions.

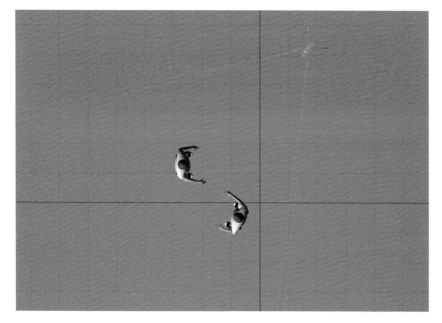

7.11 While you can just draw your plans for staging, this diagram uses 3D characters. Here, you can see the position of the camera as it is set for a two-shot.

Perhaps your scene requires more than two characters, such as three or four people. How should they be staged? Like any scene, it depends on the dialogue at hand. A setup like the one in Figure 7.12 makes a good starting ground. One camera can cover the action of two characters standing together. Another camera can cover the close-up reactions and dialogue of a single character.

7.12 A two-camera shot staged for three characters. Here, you can see that the upper-right camera can cover the dialogue of two characters, while the bottom camera focuses on a close-up of the single character.

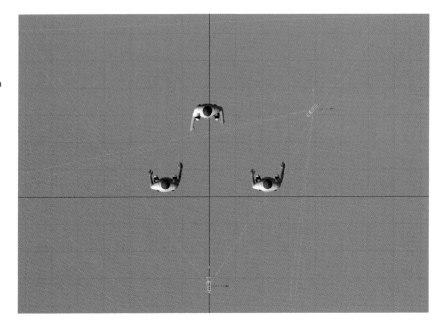

Going one step further, your scene might call for a group shot. Perhaps your animation calls for a large crowd that is having a heated discussion about a situation in which they are all involved, such as a traffic accident. You don't want the viewer to be confused by constant cutting between close-ups of people talking. The shot requires that you establish the group and remind the audience at times where each character is staged in relation to the rest of the group. Figure 7.13 shows one possible scenario.

7.13 A more complex shot with multiple characters can benefit from a staging setup like this. One camera can focus on the main character's dialogue, while the other can retain a view of the entire group.

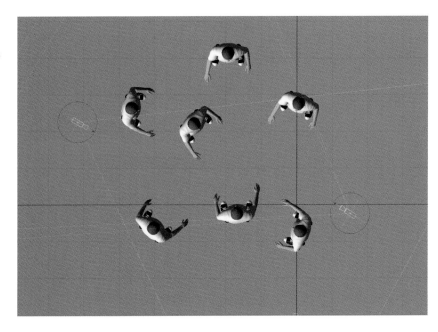

Much of the staging you'll use will work because of a combination of character placement and camera placement. Figures 7.14 through 7.17 explore various dialogue stagings. Chapter 8, "Lines of Action," will revisit setups like these when discussing camera angles.

7.14 Face-to-face, or one-on-one, dialogue shots should be staged so that the viewer can read the faces and see emotion.

7.15 One-on-one dialogues can show the characters staged next to each other.

7.16 Less casual shots between two characters can show the actors staged
slightly differently from side-by-side
shots.

7.17 Characters placed apart give the
viewer a sense of distance.

Staging digital characters in your animations relies on the variations listed here and your own personal instinct. Using these techniques, and even acting out the staging yourself, will allow you to properly stage your actors. If you're like most independent animators, however, you're not always working with digital characters. Sometimes, you're not working with characters at all. Perhaps you're working with buildings for architectural animations, machinery for industrial-type animations, or even simple product shots. How should these real-world objects be staged?

7.3 PRODUCT STAGING

While character animation is often revered as the Holy Grail of animation, you may not need to create, stage, or animate any type of character. Your work is that bread and butter stuff—logos, animated text graphics, machinery, and product shots. How can staging help you? Well, in most cases, the staging you'll need to use involves the camera more than the content. Text graphic staging really comes from the designer who creates and aligns the text. How your viewers see it relies on camera angles, lenses, and motion.

Product shots, on the other hand, still need proper placement. Setting up a good single product shot is nothing more than placing the product on a set or photographer's *cyc*, or cyclorama, and making sure that the subject is properly lit and framed. A cyc is nothing more than a backdrop which extends behind and beneath a character or product. Have you ever been to a photographer's studio and seen them pull down a long piece of fabric from the ceiling for you to stand on while having your picture taken? That's a cyc. Figure 7.18 shows a single product shot.

What if you have more than one product? What makes inanimate objects appear balanced and pleasing to the eye? How do you decide where to position the objects on your set? The answers are often found right before your eyes—just look at the scene at hand. Ask yourself if the shot is aesthetically pleasing. Does it feel good? That might sound crazy, but any shot you set up should "feel" right. What makes a shot feel right? Things such as proper balance—is the shot set up properly, or is there too much head room? Perhaps the product is partially cut from view? Make sure the shot is positioned well. Other things that make shots feel right are proper lighting and shadows. Shadows give a sense of depth and realism to 3D renders, but they should not obscure the

7.18 Staging products for animation is important to the digital director. Here, a model car is positioned to highlight the sale of a new model sedan.

product. Make sure a shadow from, for example, a back light does not overpower the main light source. Other aesthetic considerations can be proper color and properly scaled geometry. Perhaps you're creating a product shot of a desk. Everything is in place: the phone, the lamp, and the coffee mug. But the mug is half the size of the lamp! Make sure your objects are properly sized so that their relationship to other objects is well balanced.

You can study film, video, or art for years, but if the final shot just doesn't feel right, then what's the point? There is, of course, another aspect to consider when staging products, and that's the product itself. That is to say, what are you trying to convey in the shot? What's important? Just as you want viewers to see the body language and emotion in shots with digital characters, you want your viewer to be able to identify the products in these shots. Figures 7.19 and 7.20 show two variations on product placement.

Staging is important throughout your digital work. It's especially important for placement of your digital characters so that their body language and emotion are evident to the viewer. Beyond that, staging can be applied to such inanimate objects as automobiles, products, or machinery.

7.19 Some types of products might need to be clearly seen so the viewer knows what the client is selling.

7.20 You can set up product shots simply to highlight a piece of equipment. Multiple copies of the object can serve as accent pieces for a more complete shot.

7.4 BLOCKING

Any discussion of staging should incorporate blocking, also called *z-axis blocking* in some 3D software. *Blocking*, like staging, is the choreographed movement of the digital actors or camera. The difference is that blocking uses these elements to add interest and break up a shot. Once you've staged your characters, you can use blocking techniques to create a more creative shot, such as an obscure character walking right in front of the camera lens. Blocking is a film term that's been used cinematically for years. But with the advent of computer graphics and imaging, you can use not just the term, but also the method in your computer-generated images.

Too often, animators tend to stage characters or props along the same axis. For example, you're shooting a street scene, and your characters are all lined up along a sidewalk. An average shot would show these characters from shoulder height, clear and straight as if you were another person standing there, watching. But this is boring. You can employ blocking techniques to add interest and depth to your scenes. Figure 7.21 shows a render of a street scene with characters viewed from a standard vantage point. Figure 7.22 shows the same shot utilizing blocking. Figure 7.22's shot has a character viewed close up, while the same wide shot in Figure 7.21 puts him in the background.

7.21 A typical shot shows characters lined up all on the same axis. Their positions from the camera remain the same. The shot is ordinary. But you're working in a digital environment, and you should take advantage of the power at your fingertips. You can set up any shot the way you want!

7.22 A shot with blocking has more depth and interest. Here, a figure can be seen close up while the character in the backdrop remains in a full shot. You can use depth of field to emphasize the shot as well.

Staging and blocking are techniques to which you should consciously pay attention. Study, practice, and understand how and why these techniques are used. From there, positioning your subjects should come naturally, and your focus should be your story and your animation. Blocking and staging always happen—simply pointing your 3D camera at a subject is blocking and staging—but good blocking and staging consists of these elements:

- Points of interest
- The viewer's point of view
- A character's point of view
- Lines of action, such as camera angles and composition

When you read through the other chapters in this book on topics such as composition and camera angles, think of how those topics relate to blocking and staging.

NOTE

Blocking in 3D animation is sometimes referred to as z-axis blocking.

7.4.1 ILLUSION OF DEPTH

The techniques described in this chapter are all based on traditional cinematic principles. In the computer animation environment, you have more control than everyday filmmakers who are constantly battling light, equipment, and talent to bring forth their visions. The vision should be fraught with feeling, emotion, body language, energy, and depth. Depth is a misleading word that often makes animators think of deep focused shots or camera tricks. On a larger scale, depth in blocking and staging allows you to involve more in a frame by including necessary foreground and background subjects, hence the illusion.

In addition, depth adds emotion to a scene. Depth does this by using scale, and it often creates more than one meaning for a shot. For example, a shot of a photographer preparing his camera in the foreground, while an unsuspecting movie star is walking toward you in the background, tells you that the movie star will soon have a paparazzo in her face who will be taking a surprise photograph. And, he'll probably sell it the next day for $100,000 to a tabloid. Techniques for creating greater illusion of depth in your animations can be achieved with macro lenses and focus adjustments. For example, how do you portray to the viewer just how small a bug is on a leaf? How is the viewer to know that this is not a life-size bug? You need to portray an illusion of depth. To do so, you can create a significant depth of field. Using a close-up shot of the bug while the surrounding areas and even parts of the bug are out of focus creates the illusion that the out-of-focus areas are much larger. Take a look at a photograph of a tiny object, such as a bug, or perhaps a close-up of a wristwatch. The focus is clear on the object, but unclear elsewhere. The illusion to the viewer is depth. Here are a few guidelines to follow:

- Define the relationship of your subject to the surrounding environment.

- Use depth of field for added realism.

- The more out of focus the surrounding environment is, the greater the illusion of depth.

- Large elements in view, such as half a frame of a character in profile looking down a long, busy city street, can create a strong illusion of depth.

- Get the camera off the shoulder! As in many video production studios, 3D animators often leave the camera at fixed and general heights. Move the camera to a bird's-eye or bug's-eye view for added illusion of depth.

7.4.2 THE RULE OF THIRDS

A technique that can help you visualize your shots is the *rule of thirds*. The rule of thirds means to view your shot through a grid made up of three equal parts, both vertically and horizontally. This rule is a basic principle often used in photography, video, and film. As a matter of fact, there are lenses you can buy for cameras that make this rule visible through a viewfinder. The rule of thirds involves the four convergence points where these grid lines intersect. This is where your eye automatically goes to first, and any object of interest placed in that position will seem to be framed properly.

The rule of thirds really applies to camera shots and cinematography, and it is the job of the director of photography. But it's mentioned here with staging because it is something that can help you when staging and blocking your shots, as it allows you to visualize where to place your characters and subjects.

This book is about perspective and vision—your vision. The tools to get you there are at your fingertips, and the information here guides you along the way. The rule of thirds is an additional visual element that you can use not only to set up your shots and compose a frame, but also to better stage your characters and props. Beyond staging characters, the rule of thirds can help you even more by helping stage an entire scene that might include cars or buildings. Figure 7.23 shows an example of the book's cityscape shot with a grid made in thirds painted over.

7.23 The rule of thirds is a visual reference you can think of when setting up shots. It can be used for staging, blocking, or composition.

Keep practicing it, and the rule of thirds will start to work itself into each of your shots. You'll set up shots within each third without even thinking about it. Figure 7.23 shows a city scene that was not initially thought about in thirds. When the grid was painted over it, the '67 Chevy Impala fell within one area of the grid, while the upper portion of the el train tracks have worked their way into a third, while sets of buildings on the left side of the frame fall within two of the thirds.

Not every element needs to be placed within a third or a square—that's not how it works. The idea behind using the rule of thirds is that you can frame your shots and character positions better. For example, Figure 7.23 shows the buildings on the left falling within two left thirds of the screen. Notice, however, that a few of the buildings at the back of the shot move into the right third of the frame. The '67 Impala will undoubtedly move from its third box to another during the animation. But the goal is that your initial shot has balance with the other elements and surroundings. Drawing on a blank sheet of paper is hard for some people, while others just work better with graph paper. Adobe Photoshop and other imaging programs have an overlay grid you can turn on to line up your graphics. Visualizing your shots in thirds is like adding graph paper over your camera lens, allowing you to align and balance subjects. In order to know if you are using the rule of thirds properly, think of sight lines or readings. When you are presented with a new image, for example, the eye goes to the most prominent shape in the frame, which is called the *first read*. Then the eye wanders to a secondary shape, the *second read*, and so on. Care should be taken when staging to make the most important thing in your shot, such as your characters or a '67 Impala, the most prominent object in the shot and therefore as first read. Otherwise, it might get lost in a busy background.

7.5 THE NEXT STEP

Your 3D animation software is your own personal stage. You can act out your dreams, fears, or fantasies without leaving your office. The power of your software enables you to mimic reality, and often, what is not reality.

You need to practice and learn where to place your characters and subjects, as well as understand how they should interact with one another. Staging is a technique among many others that you should use when creating 3D animation. While it's more important for animations dealing with characters and dialogues, the techniques can be beneficial to even the industrial animator and illustrator. Staging is important to allow the viewer to understand what is important and what isn't. It enables character's emotions and body language to be as much a part of the scene as the dialogue, sets, and sound.

The following chapters will take you to the next step: exploring camera angles and composition, as well as audio and digital post production.

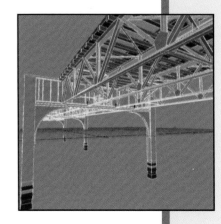

[CHAPTER] 8

LINES OF ACTION

A LINE OF ACTION is a visual element that you should look for in digital cinematography and directing. It is a strong line that you can follow through your character. The opening image for this chapter shows a single dancer posed on a set. There is a strong line of action from her feet through her hands. Line of action has to do with the aesthetically pleasing aspect discussed earlier in the book. It is something the viewer is not necessarily conscious of, but the human eye will pick up on strong, and consequently, weak lines of action.

Lines of action are important to your characters and your shots. Not only should your characters be posed properly with a good line of action, so should your camera. Properly setting up shots and using the right camera angles where appropriate is what will make or break a shot. This chapter will discuss the many possible camera angles you can use and when you should use them, as well as shot continuity and composition.

8.1 BASIC CAMERA ANGLES

The camera angle is defined by subject size, subject angle, and camera height. There are three types of camera angles, each with many variations of framing depending on the three defining factors:

- Point-of-view angles

- Subjective angles

- Objective angles

Shots using *point-of-view angles* appear to be looking from the viewpoint of a character, such as a bug walking across a counter. *Subjective angles* are personal; they bring the viewer into the shot. For example, a speeding car appears to be going fast from an outsider's view, but a shot from within the car or alongside the bumper puts the viewer in the role of passenger and creates a greater visual experience for the viewer. *Objective angles* are shots from the sidelines and are sometimes called the *audience point of view*. With an objective shot, the viewer is less involved and more of a voyeur.

What the camera sees is a matter of subjects and space. The role of an actual camera angle is meaningless without subject matter. How the subject matter is viewed is important to developing a story, mood, character, or scene. The camera has perspective, and in the digital realm, you have control over it, as you do in the real world. When preparing your shots, a good idea is to set up your camera with low-resolution copies of your subjects. Perform any staging or blocking, and get a feel for how the scene will work. You can replace the low-resolution 3D elements with the final high-resolution models when it's time to render. (See Figure 8.1.) This method can help you determine the right camera angles. The subject matter will eventually determine the final shot, such as a two-shot or wide establishing shot, but planning your camera angles beforehand can help you concentrate solely on the shot first.

Camera angles can make or break a shot. A motion picture, short film, or 3D animation is composed of many shots. Each shot requires placement of the camera for the best possible situation for seeing the actors and sets. A carefully positioned camera and the camera angle establish both the viewpoint and the area covered in the shot. The way you place the camera in your 3D work is subjective. Like your 35mm camera, the 3D camera is personal, and your viewer joins your vision. The camera is the eye of the viewer in each and every scene.

8.1 Preparing your camera angles can be made easier by first working with the camera and simple, stand-in low-polygon objects before final-high resolution subjects are placed in the shot. This makes camera setup quick and easy.

Full shots, medium shots, and close-up shots are just the starting ground for you. There are many shots you can use for all types of situations. Additionally, you can employ variations of focus, movements, and lenses. To help you sort out all your options, you should first learn about framing.

8.2 FRAMING

When you setup your animations, you have the option to shoot the scene any way you like. The framing you choose can bring the viewer closer or farther from involvement and intimacy with the characters or subjects. Framing, either open or closed, allows you to include or exclude the viewer from the rendered image. *Open-framed shots* involve things that are usually beyond the filmmaker's control, such as scenery, birds in the sky, or large crowd scenes. *Closed-framed shots,* however, are scenes with very deliberate and careful placement of subjects and props. Now if you think about it, everything you create in your computer software is deliberately and carefully placed, so your framing is really always closed. This is one area that differs from the traditional film-making world.

Framing your shots means understanding and also using the lenses you have available in your 3D package, which are all real-world lenses and then some, when working in the computer environment. Filmmakers often try multiple closed-framing options to decide what looks best for the scene at hand. For the computerized cinematographer, you can either set up multiple cameras or move a single camera to view your shots as needed. Figure 8.2 shows an overview render of a 3D bedroom that is framed with multiple cameras. Figures 8.3 through 8.5 show the renders from the different cameras.

8.2 An overview of a 3D scene shows how multiple cameras can be used to set up differently framed shots.

8.3 Viewed from above, this camera angle can act as a voyeuristic or spy cam. An overview like this is also good for establishing the set.

8.4 A lower-angle shot at the foot of the bed brings the viewer to a specific point of interest, while keeping a slight view of the open doorway in the back.

8.5 At a bug's-eye view, and also outside of the room, this camera angle is more dramatic.

Framing your shots relies on your ability to make the view aesthetically pleasing and balanced. For example, Figure 8.6 shows a character well balanced and properly framed for a comfortable-looking shot. He is looking into the frame, which allows the viewer to see his face and read his emotions and reactions.

Figure 8.7, on the other hand, shows a variation of the shot with the subject now facing away at the edge of the frame. The image is uncomfortable because the character's view appears blocked. The viewer has no idea what the character is seeing, and the shot is uneasy. This does not make the shot bad, depending on the story that's being told. Uncomfortable shots that leave you wondering, as this one does, can create

8.6 This simple shot of a character is well balanced and comfortable as the figure is facing into the frame.

8.7 A poorly framed shot can be uncomfortable for the viewer. There is slightly too much space (head room) above the figure, and he is looking at the edge of the frame, not allowing viewers to know what he's seeing.

interest if the story or segment at hand calls for it. However, if this character were having a dialogue with someone, the shot would be poorly framed because you couldn't see to whom or what the person was talking.

You can see from the previous examples that framing shots can make a large impact in how the shot looks and feels. In addition to the camera angle, a properly framed shot takes into account the subject angle and camera height.

8.2.1 SUBJECT ANGLE

Some 3D animators consider the angle of the camera only and not the subject. While the subject angle is important to staging, as discussed in Chapter 7, it is equally important to your camera. How the camera views a subject's angle can add or decrease depth in a shot. Traditional filmmaking and 3D animation both involve height, width, and depth. Characters, sets, props, and more all have a top, front, back, bottom, and sides. These need to be considered in every shot. For example, Figure 8.8 shows a shot with a straight vertical line of action. The bookshelf is flat and lacks depth, even though there is more to the 3D model. You only see the height and width, but no depth.

8.8 A shot that is viewed straight on lacks depth. (Image courtesy of Rob Maxwell.)

Figure 8.9 shows the same shot viewed with from a different angle. Now the shot conveys the building's depth.

Subject angle is important throughout your work, especially when dealing with the human form. The appropriate lens and subject angle will produce the best results. What determines the appropriate lens and subject angle depends greatly on the type of image you want to convey to your viewers. Let's say two characters are arguing on a city street. A fight ensues, and one character punches the other in the face. You want the viewer watching this animation to feel what that punch was like to the character. You can cut to a shot with a significant wide angle, so much so that a "fish-eye" lens is now the field of view for the character. Mix that with blurring and echoes of sound, and you can portray a character who has been knocked in the head.

Using the appropriate lens may also be based on matching real-world video. This might happen if you need to create 3D animated environments for a music video. The band was shot live on a green screen with a very wide angle lens, and it's your job to match the 3D camera to the real-world camera. You can do this by taking note of the lens and camera used to shoot the band and then applying those settings and focal lengths into your 3D application's camera controls.

8.9 With a different subject angle, the shot now has depth. (Image courtesy of Rob Maxwell.)

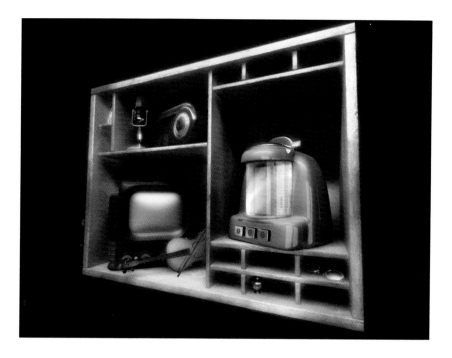

On a simpler level, achieving appropriate camera lenses and angles is a matter of subject. For example, if you need to show a large, three-story building for an architectural re-creation, a wider lens positioned low and tilted up will offer more to the viewer than a zoomed lens. Why? There are two reasons. First, a wider lens allowed you to fit more into the field of view. Second, a wider lens creates a larger feeling of scale, giving the building a more realistic look and feel. By contrast, a zoomed lens from high above could make the building look like a miniature or toy. The result you should work toward involves depth, as well as width and height.

8.2.2 CAMERA HEIGHT

If home videographers, wedding photographers, and 3D animators can be found guilty of one thing, it's the lack of camera height. More often than not, shots remain at a stationary height, such as a shoulder-level home camcorder. Animators often move the camera on the X (left and right) and Z (back and forth) plane, but do very little movement on the Y (up and down) axis. A viewer's interaction with a scene, as well as the effectiveness of the shot, relies on the camera height. You need to be careful what height you choose when setting up shots. Remember, you're working in 3D and can move the camera anywhere you want—so do it! Figures 8.10 and 8.11 show two camera height variations.

8.10 Shot with proper camera height, the view of the cityscape from above shows the expanse, depth, and length of the elevated train tracks. A shoulder- or tripod-level shot would not be as effective. This is a bird's-eye point of view.

8.11 Shot low and from a bug's- or worm's-eye point of view, buildings look ominous and their height is prevalent.

Camera height has significant impact on the viewer's involvement in the shot. It can be key to representing a particular scene of a story.

8.3 TYPES OF SHOTS

Sometimes the best way to learn is to study examples. Figure 8.12 demonstrates an establishing shot, and Figures 8.13 through 8.18 show a cityscape shot from a series of camera angle examples. To help you frame your shots, consider how the same scene can seem to change with the camera angle.

These are just some of the many choices you can use, and as you can see from these seven examples, there are many ways you can shoot a scene. Your digital cinematography techniques will vary from scene to scene, but you can use the basic examples as a starting ground. The combination of the right staging, framing, camera height, and subject angle will produce a great-looking shot.

Any of these shots can be static or moving, either by physical camera movement or the changing of lenses. But before you move the camera, you should be aware of continuity.

8.12 An *establishing shot* is essential in many productions. It defines the location, be it a large building, room, house, or even a desktop. Perhaps your animation short takes place completely in a two-room school-house. The establishing shot is what begins the animation and allows viewers to become familiar with what they are seeing and also where they are.

8.13 A *two-shot* can be beneficial when both characters' roles are equally important.

8.14 *High-angle shots* can provide the viewer with contrast and variety when watching the screen. High angles are also good for viewing bugs or small objects that are commonly below eye level.

8.15 *Low-angle shots* have been used for years to portray strength and power. Looking up at a subject like a creepy monster or mob boss makes the creature more intimidating.

8.16 *Angle-plus-angle shots* are not usually talked about, but probably are a type of shot that logo animators or architectural animators will use at some point. An angle-plus-angle shot combines an upward (or downward) angle with subject angle. The result is significant depth and an enhanced 3D experience.

8.17 A *Dutch angle* is not often used in 3D animation, but it should be! Simply rotate your camera upon its bank axis to create a Dutch-angle shot. You can use Dutch angles for odd situations or perhaps a character who is confused and bewildered. The Dutch angle will emphasize the disorientation.

NOTE

A camera's bank axis is not an up-and-down move or a left-to-right rotation, but rather a rotational value upon itself in a clockwise or counter-clockwise fashion. For example, as an airplane flies, it doesn't just turn left or right, it also banks. If a plane were to "bank left," it's left wing would dip down while the right wing would go up.

8.18 An *over the shoulder* (OTS) shot is very common for dialogue sequences.

8.4 CONTINUITY

You should always maintain continuity throughout your animation. The smooth flow that viewers see from one shot to another, continuity can keep or lose your audience. It can keep them by creating a logical progression shot after shot. They are compelled to watch because the shots make sense in their mind. You can lose viewers if continuity fails because shots are illogical, out of order, or simply inconsistent scene after scene. So what determines good continuity? How do you achieve it?

First, think about how things happen in the real world: They move forward. Your hair grows from short to long; your cup starts out full and empties as you drink it. If your short film or animation shows a character with short hair, then long hair, then short again without establishing how it got that way, such as a haircut, the viewer is confused and continuity is broken. The same can be said for a cup of coffee in a shot. In the opening scene, the waiter pours the coffee, filling the cup. A few shots later, without the actor drinking or spilling a drop, the cup magically empties!

Continuity issues such as these are less likely for the digital content creator, but should be a concern nonetheless. They are less likely because everything you are creating is fake. For example, there is no chance that if you animate a waiter filling a cup of coffee that your digital actor will spill or drink it off camera! Maintaining continuity is even more challenging when you consider that traditional filmmakers usually shoot scenes out of order and over several months. Monitoring for inconsistencies can be very difficult in that environment. But, in the computer environment, you have complete control over aging actors, coffee cups, hair styles, and more.

If your story involves a shift to an earlier point in time, you must be careful in your execution. What transports the character back in time? Simply cutting to it without a visual thought or reference will confuse the viewer, making him ask, "How did I get here?" If the character is dreaming or lost in a memory, how will the viewer know? Think about movies you've seen when a character is dreaming. What happens? The shot zooms in on the character sleeping or thinking, and the shot either blurs or an effect is added, such as wavy lines to let viewers know that a transition is taking place.

Continuity in your camera shots is just as important as the continuity of your story. Many stories begin with a narrative that allows you to understand where you are in a point in time, such as the present. The narrative describes a situation as it currently stands, and as the dialogue continues, the shots change appropriately. Perhaps the dialogue takes you back so that you can see how the situation ended up the way it did at the start of the film. This type of storytelling is effective and intriguing because it gives the viewer a need to stick around and find out what happened. Continuity is working.

You can use certain establishing shots to keep continuity within a project. For example, two passengers board a train. Viewers have already seen an establishing shot to let them know the characters are at the train station. This allows the editor to cut to a close-up of the actors to follow their action and dialogue. From here, the dialogue can continue from within the train. If the next cut has the character exiting the train at a different location than the initial establishing shot, the continuity is broken. By adding an additional establishing shot, such as a high-angle shot watching the train pass through a tunnel or through a large expanse of land, you let viewers know there is a progression, a movement in time. A shot following this with characters exiting the train now will make logical sense. One concern in traditional filmmaking is directional continuity. It's much less of a problem digitally, as changes can be made quickly, easily, and most importantly, inexpensively. Directional continuity is jeopardized any time an actor appears not to be looking directly at the other character, or a car is moving in the wrong direction. For example, if we see the mob boss driving down the street from screen right to screen left, and the police driving in their cars from screen right to screen left, one might appear to be chasing the other. But if the mob boss is moving right to left and the police are moving left to right, it might appear that there will be a collision rather than a chase. If the camera changes to view the police car from the opposite direction, it is crossing the axis of action. (More on this topic in the next section.)

Movies are made up of many different shots filmed from different cameras. Of course, you can use multiple cameras in your 3D animation program, but directional continuity is not as great of a challenge in 3D because you have ability to rehearse and change any section as needed. You can use one camera to shoot your entire animation, which often helps to eliminate directional problems. That's not to say that you can't cross the action axis because you're only using one camera. It's still possible, so you need to be aware of both the subject's motions and the camera's position to keep proper continuity. Traditional filmmakers have multiple cameras rolling and may not realize until much later that the shots don't match, that the actors were looking away from each other, or that a camera was positioned improperly. In addition, most traditional filmmakers have a continuity person whose job it is to take note and keep track of the camera's action axis. Obviously, before you render anything, you will notice if a character is not looking where it should or if the camera has moved to where it shouldn't. If a problem slips by you, you can very easily go back in and make the change.

Directional continuity often means making sure shots are similar in their actions. For example, Figure 8.19 shows two shots of a car driving down the street. Shooting the car from this same direction tells viewers that both cars are going in the same direction. Changing the camera to view one car from another vantage point might give the illusion to viewers that the car is moving in the opposite direction of the previous shot when it's really not. The camera is just looking at it from a different vantage point. Viewers will sense this awkwardness, even though the buildings and sets remain in the same position.

Continuity in 3D animation is just as important as it is in the traditional film and video world, but with a difference. Many of the continuity challenges in the traditional world come from common mistakes or changes beyond a director's control, such as a sunset—you can't control Mother Nature! In 3D, continuity issues can be focused on the story and line of action. You need not worry about the sun setting or perhaps an assistant drinking a cup of coffee and leaving it on a table in the camera's view. Work through your shots logically, and use common sense to establish that your scenes make sense.

8.19 Directional continuity must be maintained for your shots to work. Cars moving in the same direction tell the viewer one thing. If the shot changes, the viewer might think one car is moving in the reverse direction, even though the set, street, and surroundings are the same. A change in vantage point is enough to confuse the viewer and break continuity.

8.4.1 AXIS OF ACTION

To maintain continuity in your scenes, you should establish an *axis of action* in each shot. Say, for instance, the car from Figure 8.19 is driving down South Wabash Avenue in Chicago's loop. Imagine that the center yellow line in the road is the axis of action. As long as the camera never crosses this line, your shot direction will remain the same. Camera heights, pans, dollys, zooms, and so on will all work together as long as this axis line is not crossed.

Figure 8.20 shows a diagram with four cameras. As the car drives down the street, three cameras remain on one side of the axis line, which in this scene is the passenger side of the car. With this, the director can cut between the action at any point and maintain continuity. Camera 4, however, (shown in red) is positioned wrongly because, as you can see, it's opposite camera 2 across the axis of action. Cut together, these two shots would cut the axis line and break continuity. Figure 8.21 shows a simple dialogue sequence. Camera 1 provides an even plane for both characters to equally interact. Camera 2 shoots over the shoulder from the woman to view the man for his dialogue. Camera 3 shoots over the shoulder of the man to view the female's dialogue. Camera 4 is bad. It crosses the axis and breaks continuity; hence, it's crossed out in the figure.

8.20 As long as the cameras in your shot remain on one side of the axis of action, shots can maintain continuity and cut together logically.

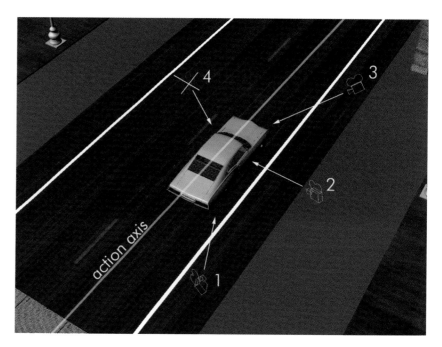

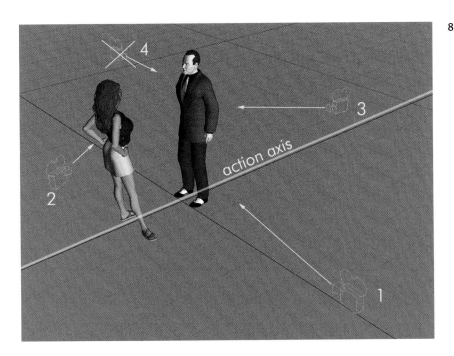

8.21 No matter what you're shooting —be it autos or dialogue—the one or many cameras in your shot should remain on one side of the axis of action.

Are there situations where the line can be crossed? Yes, but they occur more often in traditional filmmaking. A perfect scenario would be when a shot requires two actors to be filmed at different locations, but light is dominant on one side. The axis line can be crossed as long as the movement of the actor is opposite as well. Usually a pan, dolly, or overhead boom that identifies to the viewer that the axis is being crossed helps make the transition. This is not that important in 3D animation because you have control over the lighting. You don't need to worry about the sun setting or shooting in different locations. If more sunlight is needed, just add it.

In another example of axis of action, if your shot requires a dialogue scene where one character is talking on camera to a character off camera, the axis of action should still be observed. The shot can work because of the camera angles and because the cameras do not cross the axis line. That is, if the actors do their parts! Now, you've read about staging the characters, framing the shot, and maintaining continuity. Each of these is dependent on the composition of the shot. Composition in 3D animation is the artful arrangement of object within a space to create a uniform, appealing project.

An animator will compose a shot by positioning digital characters, subjects, buildings, furniture, 3D text, and so on. Good composition requires that your shots be balanced and aesthetically pleasing. Composition will vary from shot to shot because each scene you create differs in dialogue, lighting, or story. Different scenes require a different composition. And how are your scenes created? They are created with your own personal style and interpretation of story, mood, light, and more. Therefore, composition is largely a matter of personal taste.

Composition relies on what you, the animator, want your viewer to see in the shot. Many 3D content creators use 3D modeling and imaging for still print renders only. These can be for magazine covers, book illustrations, CD covers, and so on. Composition for a still image represents a visual space. When working with motion, 3D content creators are adding movement to the camera or subjects. Composition in motion represents space and time.

So what are the rules that make up good or bad composition, and how do they vary for print and motion? First, ask yourself a question: "What can I do to make this shot represent the story in the best possible way?" What is your intent for the shot? Answering these simple questions can help you compose your shots. Here are some rules by which to work:

- Use camera angles that are right for the scene at hand.

- Pay attention to continuity so that shots flow together.

- Properly use close-ups, wide angles, and establishing shots to tell a story.

- Always think about how your final production will be cut together.

- Make sure subject angles represent the mood and feeling of the scene.

Thinking visually will help produce the intended shot. Composing shots for either print or motion is not a mechanical process; rather, it is an artistic expression of your talent as a digital cinematographer and director. Although traditional filmmakers are limited to certain shots because of cables, structures, or people, digital filmmakers are unlimited in creativity. If staging, camera angles, subject angles, and continuity deal with the shape of objects and people, it's the composition that deals with the shape of the motion.

8.5 LINES OF COMPOSITION

When a camera moves within a scene, compositional lines are created, visually. The viewer's eye picks up on these compositional lines and creates a line of action, or *transitional line*. This visual line can be any combination of vertical, horizontal, straight, curved, or contoured lines. This line of composition should not divide the picture into even parts, but rather should be balanced in the frame. For example, Figure 8.22 shows a shot with a big tree. It's set smack dab in the middle of the frame. The tree cuts the composition in half. This is a poorly composed shot if the goal of the scene is to show the sunset. The viewer senses that the image is blocked and cut in half—there are now two frames to view instead of one.

8.22 Strong vertical lines should not cut the frame into even parts. The image becomes broken and unequal.

This, of course, does not mean that you can't incorporate vertical (or horizontal lines) in your frames. Strong vertical lines symbolize strength. Figure 8.23 shows the same tree composed differently. The shot is unbroken and balanced. The sunset, the goal of the shot, is visible and unobscured.

8.23 By changing the composition just slightly, the shot of the tree is balanced, unbroken, and the sunset is not blocked.

Horizontal lines work well for shots that are alike but need to be opposite of each other. For example, you've animated two characters who decide to get into an all-out snowball fight. You've set up two medium shots of each kid, one positioned left in the frame, throwing to the right of the frame. The medium shot of the other kid is positioned to the right of the frame, throwing into the left of the frame. The line of action for both kids remains the same. A visual horizontal line across the frame allows the viewer to accept the quick cuts between shots, as their level of throw is at the same height.

Parallel lines that point the viewer's eye to one direction in the distance show action, depth, and create a strong interest. Figure 8.24 shows the book's cover image: The railroad tracks in the image have strong converging lines.

8.24 Strong converging lines in a frame bring depth and interest to a shot.

8.5.1 THE TRIANGLE SYSTEM

An excellent way to compose your shots is to use the triangle system. Like the rule of thirds, which helps you frame your shots with a visual grid segmenting the frame into three equal vertical and horizontal parts, the *triangle system* is a visual reference you can look for within your shots. Figure 8.25 shows a render from an animation. Figure 8.26 shows the same image with a visual triangle drawn over it.

The triangle system in composition brings the viewer's eye from one subject to another. You don't want your viewer's eye to wander or leave the frame. Triangles can be tall or wide, such as for a landscape. A wide landscape view can be set up with a wide triangle emphasizing the width and stability of the shot. A close-up of a group of redwood trees, on the other hand, can be set up with a vertical triangle, symbolizing strength and height.

8.25 A typical shot actually has an under-lying visual element, a triangle.

8.26 The same image from Figure 8.25 shows how the triangle system allows you to visualize your composition. Notice that the lines of the triangle do not cut across a subject's face.

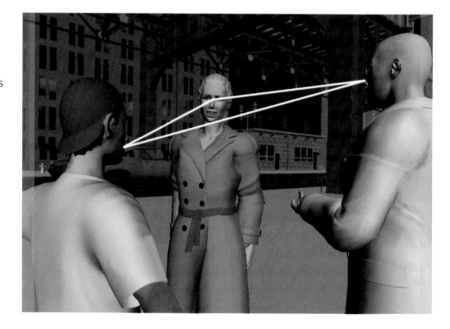

Triangles are not the only shape you can use to compose your digital shots. Circles or squares can also be used. Remember, these visual references are something that you need to look for or simply envision when setting up a shot. 3D animation packages don't offer a triangle, circle, or square overlay for scene setup. However, given that you're working in a computer environment, you easily can create a geometric object as reference, make it transparent, and attach it to your camera. Use it as a plate through which you can view your shots—sort of like training wheels for your 3D camera. Circles are helpful for framing a group of people or perhaps an architectural shot. You can create a visual circle to focus the viewers' attention on a specific subject so their eyes do not wander. When ambient light is brought to a minimum and a spotlight is used, a subject can be isolated, forcing the viewer's eye just to the lit area. The spotlight creates a circle of action. (For more on the uses of light, see Chapter 5, "Lighting.") Figure 8.27 shows an example of using a circle to focus your action.

8.27 You can use a circle as a visual reference to compose shots. Arrange your subjects that so their presence on the screen forms a visual circle similar to the layout of the subjects in Figure 8.26, which uses a triangle reference. A light source can also create a circle of action, forcing the viewer's eye to the specific subject.

You can also use letters of the alphabet to compose shots. If you visualize an L or a T, for example, your shot can be balanced in a variety of ways. The render in Figure 8.28 is framed with an "L," while Figure 8.29's shot is framed with a "T". In each, the reference lines are drawn on top for illustration.

8.28 You can use the letter "L" to frame shots. Framing with an L shape works well for digital characters, interiors, landscape shots, and more.

8.29 You can also compose shots around the letter "T," such as architectural visualizations.

Remember, these visual references are just references and guides—not steadfast rules that you need to follow strictly. Don't be a purist and force your subjects and frame to line up perfectly on a triangle, circle, or letter. By the same token, you can flip the references, such as the L. Using an L to compose a shot does not mean your composition can only have a subject on the left side of the frame. You can flip it vertically for a different shot altogether. The idea is that you follow a line of action which makes sense to the viewer. Placing subjects haphazardly and just shoving a camera on them does nothing but confuse the viewer.

Everything you've learned so far can be applied to camera movement as well. Camera movement composition adds difficulty to your shots, but you can still establish your image and work to retain those visual references throughout the shot. Using the information in Chapter 6, "[digital] Directing," you can compose shots with pans, zooms, dollys, and more. Types of movements you choose can change how the shot looks and feels for the viewer.

8.5.2 SELECTIVE FOCUSING

A good device to isolate a subject in your composition is selective focusing. Through good composition, you can deliberately push and pull the viewer's eyes to a desired subject or action. An additional way to help achieve this is through *selective focusing*. Figure 8.30 shows a shot where the focus is on the center object. Your eye goes right to it, as the blurred, out-of-focus objects seem less important.

8.30 Selective focusing and depth of field can be used to point the viewer's eye to a specific subject.

Selective focusing is nothing more than employing depth-of-field techniques in your animations. You can have a *follow focus* (or locked focus) on a subject, and as the camera follows the action, foreground objects are out of focus, keeping the viewer's eye on the subject matter. This also helps create more depth in your shots. Conversely, you can animate selective focus to change where a viewer looks. Perhaps your character is set up with a two-shot, and you've prepared the scene with creative blocking techniques. As the character in the background speaks, the camera focuses on him. When the second character in the foreground responds, the focus can change to her. In a similar scenario, if the character in the background has dialogue that's less important, or perhaps the foreground character's reactions are more important than the opposing dialogue, you can keep the selective focus on the foreground character. The sound will drive the scene, as well as the foreground character's facial reactions.

8.6 FAMILIARITY

Composing your digital scenes should be fun and kept simple. Get familiar with techniques and methods to help guide you through various setups. Get familiar with all types of movies, as well as animations. Watch what others are doing, and more importantly, what they're not doing. Pay attention at the movies or watch television to see if the shots are well balanced, are aesthetically pleasing, and allow you to follow the story. Do the shots make sense? Is there a flow? Is there continuity? Frame your shots carefully, making sure they use perspective, depth, and focus. Avoid the common straight-on, shoulder-height shots. Be creative, and don't be afraid of that camera! Move it, keyframe it, and experiment. Become familiar with how it moves, how it shoots, how it focuses, and how that all plays a role in your 3D animations.

Another strong element that plays a role in your digital cinematography and directing is audio. Audio can, and will, drive many of your shots, as well as help you visualize your shots. Read on to Chapter 9, "Sound," to learn more.

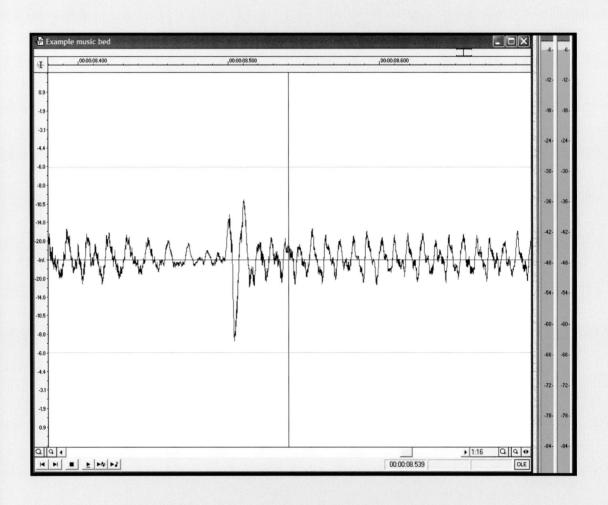

SOUND

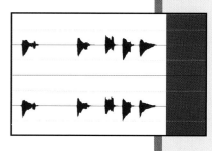

Sound

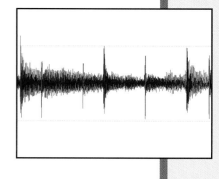

D O YOU THINK ABOUT SOUND often? As a director, you should.

For example, what would any movie be without sound? How would a science fiction film affect you if the director chose a relaxing nineteenth-century waltz for the soundtrack rather than an edgy and intense modern mix? A classic example of how sound affects the viewer is the movie *Jaws.* Just a few low notes resembling an ever-increasing heartbeat still makes audiences nervous. Can you imagine the *Indiana Jones* movies without John Williams's award-winning score to perfectly match the mood of the shots and feelings of the actors? Sound is always important, regardless of whether you're dealing with digital or traditional filmmaking. Sound is, after all, 50 percent of the term "A/V." Even if you're doing a digital short, there are always instances where the sound drives the image.

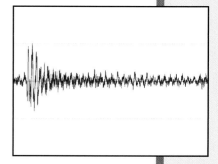

You can be sure audio is yet another element you can use to enhance and complete every shot you create. It is another subject that you can direct throughout your work. By the same token, the lack of sound (silence) can be used as effectively as a full orchestra. Silence is a great way to create tension, for example.

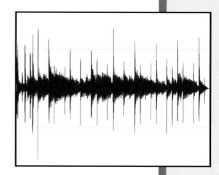

You are more than just an animator. You are a digital content creator, which means that you need to use all the tools available to you to complete your projects. Audio is a major component. Digital audio stores quite a bit of information—more than most people realize. Two key elements are sample rate and bit depth.

9.1 SAMPLE RATES AND FREQUENCY

Sample rates in digital audio are measurements of a sound's *amplitude*. This measurement happens at a short moment in time and appears as varying peaks and valleys in most digital audio editing programs. When a sound wave in your computer plays, it moves through the peaks and valleys and records how far each moves from the midpoint. The further that distance is, the greater the amplitude. When you capture audio in a computer or digital recorder, thousands of *samples* are being recorded.

Digital audio is made of lots of tiny snapshots that happen many times a second. The size of the individual snapshot is identified as the number of bits that are stored in a single digital word. The number of times in each second that a snapshot is taken is identified as the *sampling rate*. You can look at digital audio as a sort of movie. Think of the individual snapshots as frames that go by fast enough to make the images appear to move, like a film projector. The rate at which the frames go by in this movie is the *frames per second* (fps).

The *bits* are pieces of each word, called a *sample*. In a CD player, there are 44,100 16-bit samples of the audio per second, and there are two streams for stereophonic playback. This makes for a sampling rate that is called stereo 16-bit 44.1 kHz (k = 1000, Hz = cycles per second). To make it more clear, remember that a bit, or digital word, is a snapshot, or a single frame in a movie. Going a step further, bit depth or word length is the actual size of the snapshot. From there, the sampling rate consists of the frames per second of the digital snapshots that play together to reproduce a sound.

But why are there so many different formats? Most electronic devices have varying formats and standards because they are developed by different companies for different users. The most commonly used format for stereo digital audio in the home is the CD audio format. CD audio is formatted as stereo 16-bit 44.1 kHz sampling rate. But what other formats are there? Table 9.1 is a list of common digital audio formats with their bit depths and sampling rates:

TABLE 9.1

COMMON AUDIO FORMATS

Format	Bit Depth	Sampling Rate
CD Audio (stereo)	16 bits	44.1 kHz
DAT (stereo)	16 bits	48 kHz (most can also use 44.1 kHz)
DAT (extended play)	16 bits	32 kHz
MiniDisc (compressed)	16 bits	48 kHz
MiniDisc (extended play)	16 bits	32 kHz
ADAT XT (black face)	16 bits	48 kHz
ADAT XT20	20 bits	48 kHz
DVD Audio (projected)	24 bits	96 kHz
Pro MO disk	24 bits	96 kHz (192 kHz, 88.2 kHz also used)

Simply put, greater bit depth means higher resolution or quality and less noise in the audio signal. Additionally, a higher sampling rate means a greater frequency response in the digital recorder.

The sampling rate directly affects the quality of the recording. At one-half the frequency of the sampling rate, there is a sub-harmonic generated that needs to be filtered out so that it will not be heard by the listener after digital to analog conversion. This is called the *Nyquist Frequency*. The sampling rate of 44.1 kHz for CD audio was chosen years ago because it is a little more than twice the acknowledged upper limit of human hearing: 20 kHz (20,000 cycles per second). The Nyquist Frequency oscillation occurs at 22.05 kHz when a sampling rate of 44.1 kHz is employed. Often, a steep filter is employed in typical CD players and DAT (digital audio tape) recorders that allows frequencies up to 20 kHz to pass through, while almost completely filtering out the 22.05 kHz oscillations. While this all sounds quite technical, what it means to the common listener is that they are able to hear the full 20 Hz to 20 kHz audio band, while the Nyquist Frequency remains inaudible.

NOTE

The human ear can hear frequencies from as low as 20Hz up to 20,000Hz, which is the equivalent of 20kHz. Sounds from a low bass are heard in the 20Hz range. But this sound is not so much heard as it is felt. When you listen to a sound system with a sub-woofer, you feel the sound because of the low frequencies. On the opposite end, cymbals, certain vocals, and even acoustic guitars range in the 20kHz frequency range. This higher range audio is more heard than felt.

When you compress an audio file, you generally have options as to the desired kHz. While 44.1kHz sounds best, of course, it takes up the most file size. Most computer systems work with WAV files, which are recorded at 11kHz or 11,000 samples per second.

9.1.1 BIT DEPTH

The quality of the audio you sample within the computer is called the *bit depth*. Essentially, it determines the variations of volumes that a sample can reproduce. You may have seen settings in your video editing or audio program for 16-bit, 20-bit, or 24-bit. This bit depth is much like an image file's bit depth: The more there is, the better the quality. When it comes to compressing audio files, avoid extremes, such as 8-bit (poorest quality depth) and 24-bit (highest quality depth). Maintaining a quality bit depth is important because sound is so dynamic. More bit depth in your audio will enable more variations of sounds to be heard. A good bit depth to work in is about 16-bit. A 16-bit audio maintains enough quality without too much compression, producing a clean and rich sound.

9.2 SOUND AND PICTURE

In the world of traditional filmmaking, sound enhancements are typically performed after a production has wrapped. However, audio considerations need to be made during shooting as well, since you are recording source audio. Sound recording can be actors speaking, room tones, or natural sounds. After production wraps up, music, sound effects, and Foley are performed. Part of determining the locations in which you will shoot is the issue of whether the area is quiet enough, if you are shooting a dialogue-intensive scene. Of course, this isn't a necessary consideration for computer-generated animation, unless there are real-life elements within your project.

Scoring a movie, adding sound effects, loops for voice-over work, and Foley (for added realism) are part of post production. *Foley* is the art of the realistic sounds not often recorded during a shoot. These sounds can be heels walking, water pouring from a pitcher, or city traffic noise in the background. Foley artists, in many ways, are like effects artists. If you don't notice their work, they've done their job successfully. That is to say, the work is believable and seamless—completing the production instead of detracting from it.

If you talk with many composers and audio people, they might tell you that when they see a picture, be it still, moving, or animated, they begin to "hear" the music to fit the image. By the same token, many photographers, filmmakers, and animators often have visions when they hear certain music. Both scenarios are a bonus to the viewer.

For you, put on some music you like, listen, and think. That's right, think about what you see. Most people tend to have memories, thoughts, or visions when listening to music. Being a top-notch digital cinematographer and director means being able to bring your vision to the screen. What do you see? What do you feel when you hear the music? Jot down some notes, perhaps make some sketches, and get animating! Letting the audio guide the picture is yet another way that you can design and create your vision. Without sound, even just a single note extended over time, animation is not living up to its full potential. Audio is everything. You can make your pictures come alive with the right audio. The most appropriate sounds and special audio effects often can make or break your animation work.

So where should you begin? Many animation programs allow you to import audio as WAV files. Also, there are many free and very inexpensive audio editing programs available, often downloadable from the Internet. Even though WAV files are most common, there are other popular digital audio formats, such as MP3, AIFF, AU, CD, Windows Media, Real Audio, and QuickTime. You can find various audio programs that handle these formats as well as other formats at **www.digitalexperience.com/recsoft.html**. Get your hands on some digital audio recording software, and use it to both edit and time your music. One of the best applications on the market is Pro Tools from DigiDesign (**www.digidesign.com**). When you work through any audio in digital recording software, look for those peaks and valleys mentioned earlier, and discover the sounds at those points. Time the music to certain beats, and make note. This is something you can do during a preliminary edit. For example, you can create simple animatics, or still images, representing your production. With a rough idea of tempo, you can make a rough edit of what your project will look like. Use that information when keyframing your animations so the actions can be timed to the music in post production. You can use the audio directly in your animation program as well, perhaps as a guide for the lip sync of a talking character. How in the world could you make a character talk without an audio file?

Timing sounds is also a great way to estimate realistic movements. For example, your character is walking through a forest on a fall day. You just happen to find the sound of footsteps crunching leaves during a walk. As you listen to it, you picture the scene. From there, you can time the sound of the walk and keyframe your character. Maybe during this walk, a tree falls to the ground. How would you know what sort of timing to use? Audio can be a guide to the crashing sound, as well as the secondary sounds, such as branches breaking or the flutter of birds. Hearing and understanding these sounds before you animate will help generate the right kind of shot.

9.3 THE NEXT STEP

Try exercising your audio talents. For example, create an ambient bed of a particular sound. Play it over and over again as you visualize your shots. This ambient, or environmental, sound should put you in the proper emotional framework to create images that fit the sound. If you have an action scene and are not quite sure how to shoot it, find the music that could work well for that scene, then listen to it to plan your shots. The same can be said for emotional scenes, key dialogues, and more. Visualize!

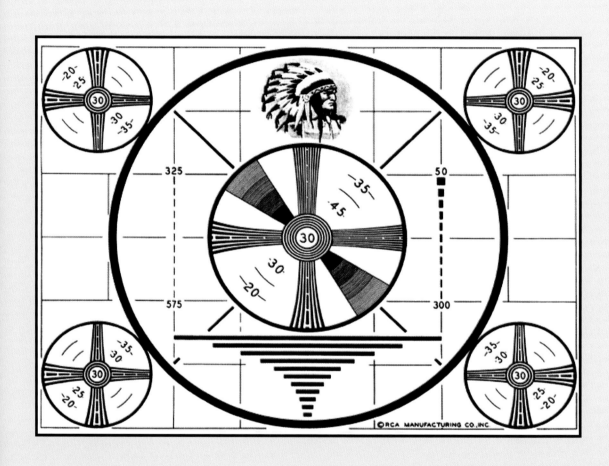

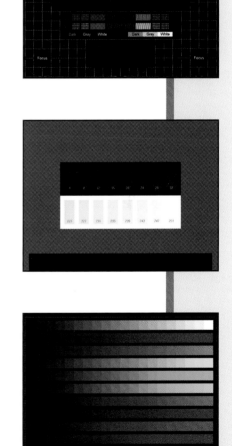

CHAPTER 10

RESOLUTIONS, COMPRESSION, AND RENDERING

TRADITIONAL FILMMAKERS, producers, and directors have a very full plate when creating their masterpieces. As the digital revolution rolls on, what were concerns and problems in the traditional world become no-brainers with a click of the mouse. For everything that is easier on the computer, however, digital filmmaking brings some new headaches that traditional filmmakers do not have to deal with, such as resolution, compression for digital content, and rendering. These headaches come from meeting two goals: keeping the quality high enough and keeping the file size small enough.

10.1 RESOLUTIONS

Not usually thought about on movie sets, resolution is a key concern for digital content creators. Not only do you need to understand your choices for aspect ratios (see Chapter 2, "The [digital] Camera"), you also need to understand the role of resolution. Television sets in the United States use a resolution of 525 *scan lines*, which is called the NTSC standard. Most European countries follow the PAL standard, which is 625 scan lines. For this to make sense, you need to understand a little about how a television display works. Perhaps you have seen a mosaic picture, where many tiny tiles of varied colors are combined to form a picture when viewed from a distance. This is a good way to begin to understand resolution. When the size of each little tile is fairly big compared to the size of the whole picture, the picture is fairly crude and cannot portray small details of the scene. Given that, when smaller tiles are used, outlines of objects in the picture become smoother and more refined, and details become more visible. The number of tiles used in the height and width of the picture is what constitutes its resolution.

When you create pictures with an electronic printer or view them on a television or computer monitor, you are working with mosaics, but you are using ink dots or phosphor elements instead of tiles. In printing, it's referred to as the count of ink dots per inch (dpi), or on video screens as pixel counts. A pixel, or picture element, is similar to a mosaic; the smaller and more numerous the pixels, the finer the resolution of the picture they can display. Home televisions sets were created on a standard resolution of 720 pixels wide, but 486 pixels tall (for NTSC, US). This simply means there are 720 pixels horizontally and 486 pixels from top to bottom. Enlarging a picture does not increase the resolution—contrary to popular belief—it only makes each pixel larger. To increase resolution, you must increase the number of pixels a picture contains. You can do this by making them relatively smaller when generating the file, which means rendering a larger image, say 1024 by 768. Once a picture is produced as a pixilated file, you cannot increase its resolution, but you can convert it to a lesser resolution.

It is important to understand that there is a significant difference between video formats and print. The pixels for video are not square; they are rectangular. The ratio varies depending on the video format, but if you need to create an image for D-1 NTSC in Photoshop or another image paint program that doesn't allow you to change the ratio of height to width in pixels, you need to work on 720 by 540, then squash the image down to 720 by 486 before saving it. Many newcomers to computer graphics are frustrated when they first confront this problem because not much information about it is readily available. Table 10.1 can help as reference.

TABLE 10.1

VIDEO PICTURE FORMATS (MEASURES ARE IN PIXELS)

Format	CCIR 601	Active Pixels	Pixel Ratio
PAL 4/3	720 × 576	720 × 576	1/1,08.
16/9 squeezed	720 × 576	720 × 576	1/1,42.
1/1,66	720 × 576	720 × 470	1/1,08
1/1,85	720 × 576	720 × 420	1/1,08
1/1,77 (16/9)	720 × 576	720 × 440	1/1,08
Format	Square Pixels	Active Pixels	Image Ratio
PAL 4/3	768 × 576	768 × 576	1/1,33.
16/9 squeezed	1024 × 576	1024 × 576	1/1,77.
1/1,66	768 × 576	768 × 470	1/1,66
1/1,85	768 × 576	768 × 420	1/1,85
1/1,77 (16/9)	768 × 576	768 × 440	1/1,77
Video to file / File to video output			
PAL 4/3		720 × 576	
16/9		720 × 576	
4/3 (square pixels)		780 × 576	
16/9 (square pixels)		1024 × 576	

Video is a series of static pictures flashing at a rapid rate. Have your eyes ever become tired looking at a television or computer monitor? Your eye is controlled by a muscle, and even though you're not conscious of the picture's flashing, your eye, and the muscle controlling it, perceives the flashing when you look at the screen. The video image you see is formed by an electronic beam that draws, or *scans*, horizontal lines from left to right, then top to bottom. The number of these horizontal scan lines determines the vertical resolution (525 lines for NTSC, 625 for PAL). In reality, only about half of those lines are displayed at any one time because television tubes are *interlaced*, meaning the scan lines are drawn in two alternating batches roughly 1/60th of a second apart—all the odd lines at once and all the even lines in another batch.

10.1 Here, you can see a listing of the various resolutions for different television formats.

VHS and 8-mm VCRs	240
U-matic (3/4-inch) VCRs	250
U-matic SP VCRs	330
NTSC Broadcast Signal	330
S-VHS and Hi8 VCRs	400
Laserdisc	425
DVD Video	500
DV Formats	500

10.1.1 COMPUTER RESOLUTION

In the computer environment, resolution is similar, but different. It's similar in that resolution is still measured in terms of horizontal and vertical resolution. But it's different in that those resolutions are much higher than in NTSC video, commonly ranging from 640×480 to 1024×768. Computer screen resolutions are measured in pixels: 640×480 means 640 pixels wide (horizontal resolution) by 480 pixels tall (vertical resolution).

Larger resolutions on your computer screen do not always mean a better picture, just a larger one. Remember the motto: garbage in, garbage out. If you scan an image into your computer at 100×200 pixels, don't expect to enlarge it to 1280×1024 pixels and think it will still be as clean and sharp as when you scanned it. Increasing the size of the image enlarges the pixels that make up the image. The result is a larger image with less pixel depth—less detail. By resizing that 100×200 image, you're actually decreasing its quality.

Computers also use a dots per inch measurement, but only when it refers to print work. Video and 3D animation work in pixels. Many times, animators render out a 3000 by 2000 pixel image, bring it into their imaging program, and it reads 72 dpi. This is inaccurate because the resolution is created for pixels, not dpi. Video translated into the computer is not 72 dpi as the 72 dpi that you get in, say, Adobe Photoshop. It is simply this value because there is no associated per-inch resolution embedded in the rendered image file, therefore Photoshop simply assigns a default dpi to the image. Think of it more as a setting for inputting and outputting—how many pixels do you want to assign to each inch or the paper, whether it is for scanning in or printing out? Video technology shows a pixel one for one, but 72 dpi in the computer is really about the size of a postage stamp. For example, a photo that is 6 × 4 inches scanned into the computer at 110 dpi equals 660 × 440 pixels.

Image quality for your digital content is something you need to monitor. If you are composing a complete digital creation, you can render at any resolution you want. That is, making sure your 3D models have enough polygonal detail. If you're going to print, you can render at resolutions up to 8000 × 8000 pixels or more! However, if you're using video footage within your creations, or perhaps scanned images or textures, you need to pay close attention to the resolution and image quality. For example, your client needs a 2000 × 3000 pixel image for a poster print. You need a logo for one section of the 3D render. All you can find is a small compressed image file from the web, so you use it. This tiny 300 × 300 sized image rendered in a 2000 × 3000 pixel image will look pixilated or blurry. So if you're going to scan in textures, image maps, or even just photos, be sure to scan at resolutions around 300 dpi or higher for the best image quality.

10.1.2 INTERLACING

You've probably seen the button in your computer's render or camera panel. Perhaps you've turned it on, not really knowing what it was for. *Interlacing* is a video term that basically means video is laid down on a display in two fields to make up one frame of video. So your animation with 30 frames per second is displayed at 60 fields of video per second. One field is comprised of all the odd scan lines and the other of all the even scan lines. First all the lines of one field are drawn top to bottom, then all the lines of the second field. Non-interlaced displays draw the video image one line after the other, top to bottom—this is referred to as *progressive*.

> **NOTE**
>
> Sharpness is due to less motion blur, which in turn is due to a faster shutter speed. Aside from the fact that the faster shutter speed is forced by having to sample the CCD 60 times a second, there really is no relation between interlaced producing sharper images than progressive.

So, if you turn on interlacing or field rendering when you output your animation, you'll have clearer, sharper pictures. This is ideal for fast-moving objects that need to retain detail in the render. One way to imagine how this looks is to picture how a high-speed shutter looks on video. Have you ever watched sport commercials or football games on television? Notice that when the players move or run, they remain sharp and clear. This is interlaced, or fielded, video. If interlace is not applied, animation playback will be steppy, or stuttered. Interlace will smooth out horizontal movement because of the additional in-between advances. Without interlace, the subject matter will not blur at all.

> **NOTE**
>
> With computer monitor playback, AVIs, MPEGs, MOVs, etc, can do without fields as the monitor is progressive. Film is progressive as well and shouldn't have interlacing.

When do you use interlacing or field rendering? It all depends on the look you want to achieve and the output device in question. Are you creating flying logos for corporate video? Are you creating detailed medical animations or walkthrough architectural visualizations? If you are creating a project for a television monitor, rendering with interlacing or fields is the choice for you. If you're compositing, matching real-world video with 3D elements, or perhaps creating digital character shorts and there is a large amount of horizontal movement you should render in noninterlaced mode (no fields). If you're rendering with noninterlaced settings, apply a little motion blur for added realism.

> **NOTE**
>
> In a production setting, you will always need to assess how long the frames for each shot will take to render. Doing so provides a reasonable estimate for full rendering that can be factored into the production timeline.

10.2 RENDERING RESOLUTIONS

Rendering is without a doubt a necessary evil. No matter how fast computer systems become, and no matter how much memory you've pumped into your system, you still end up with rendering issues. This is because as systems become more powerful, you find yourself adding more intense features, such as radiosity and caustics. When it's time to render your animation, you need to decide what resolution you'll use. To determine this, find out if you're going to video, print, or the web. From there, choose if your animation is field rendered (or interlaced), motion blurred, and what the frames per second should be. Tables 10.2 and 10.3 will help you determine which resolution to use.

TABLE 10.2

COMMON FILM RESOLUTIONS

Film Resolutions	Image Aspect	Pixel Aspect	<1K	1K	1.5K	2K	4K
35mm Full Aperture	1.33	1.00	768 × 576	1024 × 768 1024 × 778	1536 × 1152 1556 × 1182	2048 × 1536 2048 × 1556	4096 × 3072 4096 × 3112
35mm Academy	1.37	1.00		1024 × 747 914 × 666	1556 × 1134 1536 × 1119	2048 × 1494 1828 × 1332	4096 × 2987 3656 × 2664
35mm Academy Projection	1.66	1.00	512 × 307	1024 × 614 914 × 551	1536 × 921 1556 × 938	2048 × 1229 1828 × 1102	4096 × 2458 3656 × 2202
35mm 1.75:1	1.75	1.00	560 × 320	1120 × 640	1575 × 900	2048 × 1170	4096 × 2340
35mm 1.85:1	1.85	1.00	512 × 277	1024 × 554 914 × 494	1536 × 830 1556 × 841	2048 × 1107 1828 × 988	4096 × 2214 3656 × 1976
35mm 2.35:1	2.35	1.00	512 × 218	1024 × 436	1536 × 654	2048 × 871	4096 × 1743
35mm Anamorphic 2.35:1	2.35	2.00	512 × 436	1024 × 871	1536 × 1307	2048 × 1743	4096 × 3486
70mm Panavision	2.20	1.00	880 × 400	1024 × 465	1536 × 698	2048 × 931	4096 × 1862
Panavision	2.35	1.00			1536 × 653	2048 × 871 1828 × 777	4096 × 1742 3656 × 1555
70mm IMAX	1.36	1.00	512 × 375	1024 × 751	1536 × 1126	2048 × 1501	4096 × 3003
VistaVision	1.50	1.00	512 × 341	1024 × 683	1536 × 1024	2048 × 1365 1828 × 1219	4096 × 2731 3072 × 2048
Cinemascope	1.17	1.00		1024 × 872	1536 × 1307	2048 × 1743 1828 × 1556	4096 × 3487 3656 × 3112
Cinemascope	2.35	1.00			1536 × 653	2048 × 871 1828 × 777	4096 × 1742 3656 × 1555
35mm (24mm × 36mm) slide	1.50	1.00	512 × 341	1024 × 683	1536 × 1024	2048 × 1365	4096 × 2731
6cm × 6cm slide	1.00	1.00	512 × 512	1024 × 1024	1536 × 1536	2048 × 2048	4096 × 4096
4" × 5" or 8" × 10" slide	1.33	1.00	768 × 576	1024 × 768	1536 × 1152	2048 × 1536	4096 × 3072

TABLE 10.3

COMMON VIDEO RESOLUTIONS

Video Resolutions	Image Aspect	Pixel Aspect	Resolution	Frames per Second
D1 NTSC	1.33	0.90	720 × 486	30i
D1 NTSC Widescreen	1.78 (16:9)	1.20	720 × 486	30i
D2 NTSC	1.35	0.86	752 × 480	30i
D2 NTSC Widescreen	1.87	1.15	752 × 480	30i
D1 PAL	1.33	1.07	720 × 576	25i
D1 PAL Widescreen	1.78 (16:9)	1.42	720 × 576	25i
D2 PAL	1.33	1.02	752 × 576	25i
HDTV	16:9	1.00	1920 × 1080	60i,30p,24p
	16:9	1.00	1280 × 720	60p,30p,24p
	16:9 (4:3)	1.00	704 × 480	60p,60i,30p,24p
	4:3	1.00	640 × 480	60p,60i,30p,24p
VGA	1.33	1.00	640 × 480	
SVGA	1.33	1.00	800 × 600	
XGA	1.33	1.00	1024 × 768	
SXGA★	1.25	1.00	1280 × 1024	
SXGA	1.33	1.00	1280 × 960	
UXGA	1.33	1.00	1600 × 1200	

To decide on the "best" resolution for your project, you need to understand your particular software's camera or render panel and how it affects the resolution and output of your animation. Although you're developing content within the computer environment, it is still being viewed by the computer's digital camera lens. Given that, you should have already decided on what aspect ratio your production is using, such as 4:3 or 16:9 (see Chapter 2, "The [digital] Camera"). From there, you need to determine your final output medium. Is your animation going to be printed to film? Is it going to video or the web?

Your digital content requires planning, animation, direction, execution, and, of course, rendering. Planning your project also means planning your resolutions and rendering format. Are you going to render as a sequence of RGB frames? If you're going to film, perhaps this is the way to go. Or, is your animation only a test for a web-based client preview? If so, a small movie file might be all you need perhaps at 300×200 pixels. Whichever the situation, plan ahead, and be sure to leave enough time to render your animations!

10.2.1 FRAMES PER SECOND

As film runs through a camera and the lens exposes images onto the emulsion, the film is moving at a specific rate. Traditionally, film is shot at 24 frames per second. Film's 24 frames per second has a different look than video, which is shot at 30 frames per second. This is because the power grid of the US is standardized at a 60-cycle alternating current. It's very convenient to use that as a time base for video. In Europe, the power grid is using 50-cycle current, which is why PAL is 25 frames per second. Film uses 24 frames because it is the optimum balance for the persistence of vision in your eye to the economy of film stock. Most animation programs give you the option to change not only to standard frames per second settings, but any variation you choose. Changing the frame rate can completely change the look of your render. For example, 30 frames per second is typically used for video, but even though your animation is being played back on a television monitor, you can render at 15 frames per second for a different look and playback. Your animation can be rendered at whatever frame rate you like, creating a unique look. Be sure to check with your client or producer before rendering, however, to make sure the proper frame rate is set. For example, you may need to have your work printed to film, which means a different frame rate than an animation going to the web or to broadcast video. Also, be sure that the frame rate of your final animation matches any film or video clips you incorporated into the project.

10.2.2 COMPRESSION

Digital cinematography and compression go hand in hand. Many animators have a love-hate relationship with compression. Rendered animations can be very large, especially when matched with audio, but when compressed, the file becomes much smaller, often more easily played, and more easily distributable. Because compressed files are smaller, they download faster and require less disk space for storage. The more compression you have, the less quality you'll end up with. This is because compression works by dropping redundant data that your eye doesn't pick up on, which makes the file smaller. So how do you balance the need for manageable file sizes with the desire for high quality? Take heart—many levels of compression look just as good as uncompressed footage to the human eye.

Compression schemes look for information within video (which could be a rendered animation) that doesn't change from frame to frame. Frame by frame, they assess the best areas of the image to reduce, comparing the first frame of the segment with every frame after. By the same token, audio can be, and often is, compressed as well, either tied to a video or on its own. Audio compression schemes work in a similar fashion: by looking at sound bits that are similar and redundant throughout to drop them from the file.

These schemes are called *codecs*, (which means compression and decompression). All nonlinear editing systems use some sort of compression, unless it is capable of working with uncompressed (such as the Toaster2 and some HD systems). Some codecs are unique, such as Avid, but that does not mean others cannot use this codec. For example, imported video in an Avid system will be compressed using the settings the editor applies and the system's compression codec. If the animator wants to render for that specific machine, he or she can do two things: render as normal, play the animation at video quality, and record it to tape (such as BetaSP, DV, or SVHS) or install the particular codec on his or her animation system and render to a file using it. This file can be transferred to the editing system and imported directly. The benefit of using this compression codec is not so much for file size, but rather compatibility. There are many codecs available that you can use to compress and deliver your digital content. A few of the popular codecs are MPG, MPG4, Sorenson, or MJPEG. For more information on compression codecs, visit **http://online.sfsu.edu/~ralph/895/compress.html**.

After this, the rendered animation will not only be compatible, but also retain key information such as color depth or any alpha channels for digital compositing.

Your new motto—garbage in, garbage out—applies to compressing files as well. Say your client gives you a compressed video clip. Applying more compression when you import it into your digital video or animation program further degrades an already less-than-perfect image. If you then compress the final production for delivery via the web, CD, or DVD, the result will be embarrassingly awful.

Read a spec sheet or advertisement for a video card or digital video system, and you'll probably see something about 4:1:1 or 4:2:2 sampling rate. These ratios relate to video. A 4:2:2 compression means that color is sampled at half the rate of the luminance, with color remaining the same with the luminance sample. This is twice the sampling rate of a 4:1:1 compression scheme. 4:1:1 is more common to DV formats, while 4:2:2 is component (RGB). For animations, you should always work in 4:2:2 compression because it retains more information and has a larger data capacity for such effects as compositing and keying. In addition to 4:2:2 and 4:1:1, many nonlinear systems today use 3:3:1 *lossless compression* scheme. The 3:3:1 is a moderate but good-looking compression equal to DV (Digital Video) compression.

10.2.3 4:1:1 AND 4:2:2 SAMPLING RATES

In the digital world, video signals are encoded when recorded and decoded on playback. Depending on the digital format, the video signal will be sampled at either 4:1:1 or 4:2:2 sampling. The digital video signal has three components: luminance (Y), which is a color value consisting of the luminance deducted from the color red (R–Y), and the color value of the luminance deducted from the color blue (B–Y). These are the same components that make up a Betacam SP and Digital Betacam signal. These three components, Y, R–Y, and B–Y are also known as "YUV."

During the digitizing process, the three parameters of the component video signal are assigned a numeric sampling value by the system that is digitizing them. Groups of four video pixels within each of the three components are looked at, and samples are taken for recording. With a 4:2:2 sampled video signal, all four of the luminance pixels are sampled, two of the R–Y pixels are sampled, and two B–Y pixels are sampled.

This gives you a 4:2:2 sampling rate. With a 4:1:1 signal, all four of the luminance pixels are sampled four times out of four, but only one pixel is sampled from each of R–Y and B–Y. This lowers sampling rates of the color components, and it will result in less color information being recorded. This lower sampling rate affects the accuracy and intensity of the color in the video signal. You might not want to use 4:1:1 when doing chroma keying for compositing, image graphics, and other compositing functions because all of these require strong colors to be present in the video signal.

The advantage of 4:1:1 sampling is that you can record twice as much information onto the same area of video tape, which provides twice as much recording and playback time. Additionally, the circuitry within the equipment is less expensive for a manufacturer to produce. 4:1:1 is the sampling rate used with the consumer DV format, along with DVCAM and DVCPRO. The 4:2:2 sampling rate is used with Digital-S (from JVC), DVCPRO-50 (from Panasonic), Digital Betacam, D-1, and D-5. The 4:2:2 sampling rate is more common in the professional video arena.

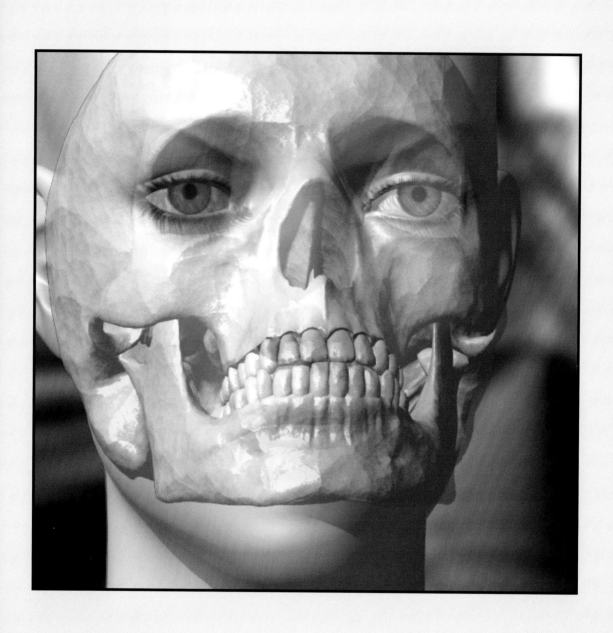

11

EDITING

E DITING HAPPENS AFTER a film has been shot or after an animation has been rendered. During this process, all of the final shots and sequences are brought together into one coherent masterpiece. Music and sound are added, as well as such additional elements as special effects or titles. Without the editing process, a film or animation is nothing more than footage. An editor is someone who can complete, and in many situations create, the visual experience for the viewer. The process involves cuts, dissolves, wipes, and transitions at precise moments between precise shots.

Editing is the final process of creating a project whether on film or in digital media, and it is the art of assembling all of the elements of sounds and images created during production into a logical, flowing presentation. The decisions that an editor makes are crucial to the success of the project. It is during the editing process that individual shots are joined together to construct each scene sequentially to reveal or present all the scenes in an order that tells a story.

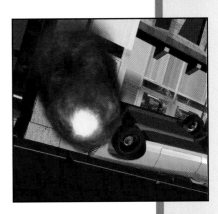

The joining of one shot to another is called a *cut*. The term originated from film production because editors literally had to cut the pieces of film to be spliced together. When two shots are simply joined together directly, it is known as a *butt-cut*, since one butts-up to the other. All the other types of joinings are called *transitions*. Transitions create many alternative ways to go from one shot to

another, such as cross-dissolves, fades, and a host of graphic manipulations such as wipes, peels, and fly-aways, all of which provide a vast array of transitions. To perform a cut or transition, each shot must be trimmed to select in-points and out-points that will optimize the joining with other shots.

Most editing techniques are concerned with creating and preserving a continuity in the presentation of the performances. Cuts and transitions are selected by the editor (and often producer) to create the best connection between shots in a scene and between scenes. However, an editor can only assemble what he has been provided with by the director and cinematographer. Editing must be planned during production in order to provide all shots essential to the plan. Remember the phrase—garbage in, garbage out!

Some shots may require compositing or other embellishments, such as color correction or re-timing for proper speed, prior to editing. Often, these processes are done in a different department and are provided to the editor ready to be integrated into the project. Also, some effects, such as layering or compositing and editorial transitions are rendered during editing, especially in digital editing. Animators often render in multiple passes, first creating a background animation, then rendering a pass with a character or two, and then rendering a beauty pass for skies, atmospheres, etc. These multiple passes are put together during the editing process. This is useful for control, as there is more room for adjustment because each element is in its own independent layer.

Editing styles have changed over the years as audiences have become more aware of digital techniques. Some styles used today would have left audiences of 1930 totally confused and bewildered. Next time you see an old movie on TV, watch how the editor led you through the story. Compare this with a modern production, perhaps such as the movie *Swordfish* or *Memento*, and you will see how much the techniques have evolved.

NOTE

It's important to note that in computer-generated feature production, the editing process often happens concurrently with the early stages of the project. The reason for this is that it's impossible to know which shots to tweak or enhance without first cutting the footage together. In this respect, computer generated feature editing is a different animal from traditional film editing—the cut is often done months before the project is actually completed. Yet basic editing principles still apply, regardless of when the edit is performed.

11.1 EDITING FOR ANIMATION

It's safe to say that once you've completed a 3D animation, digital content, or multimedia project, you'll be doing the post production in a nonlinear environment. Linear editing is done from video tape to video tape. Nonlinear editing, on the other hand, is done within a digital environment, so shots can be used over and over, as well as manipulated, without a loss of quality. In linear editing, if you want to use a shot twice, you need a copy, and then transitions need to be performed from one tape source to another. This is AB roll editing, something that really is not prevalent in a nonlinear environment. Simply put, with nonlinear editing, you'll be editing within the computer. There are many types of editing platforms, from video to film, but for the purpose of this chapter, we'll concentrate on digital editing and the techniques involved.

Editing is more than using cuts and dissolves between shots, and as such, it should be part of any animation project you create. By understanding how the editing process works, you can better assess the animation you need to create, as well as the types of shots to work toward. There is a saying that the best editors are photographers or cinematographers, and the best cinematographers are editors. What this means is that an editor knows exactly what type of shot works from cut to cut and understands the shot flow necessary to make a scene flow. By the same token, a photographer who understands the editing process also knows which shots will work together and, more importantly, which ones won't. Good photographers think ahead to how the final scene will look once edited. Your understanding of the entire cinematic process as an editor will open the doors to greater possibilities.

When you finish an animation, editing can be used to put an entire film together, but also even to cut together simple clips or loop an animation, giving it a longer life without added render hours. Believe it or not, directors and editors work hard to *avoid* showing a cut in an edit. It might sound odd, but if you think about it, the process makes sense. The goal of any animation or film is to tell a story, and if the viewer notices a poorly framed shot or a jerky edit, the flow of the story being told can be lost. This might sound extreme, but without acknowledging this fact, all of your hard work is in vain. So what makes for a good edit or a bad edit? Figure 11.1 shows an initial shot, while Figure 11.2 shows the next shot. Cut together, this edit makes a bad cut.

11.1 An initial shot of a character works well for your first edit.

11.2 Cutting to this shot right after the previous one creates a jump cut, which is a bad transition.

There are no inherently bad cuts. A cut's success or failure all depends on the type of shot and the type of story is being told when the cut is used. To understand this, take a look at the various edits you can use to put your animations together.

11.1.1 JUMP CUTS AND THE 35-DEGREE RULE

Jump cuts are sudden relocations of the camera during a scene, as if the camera suddenly jumps from one place in a scene to another. This is also known as the 35-degree rule. An edit needs to change the angle of the image by more than 35 degrees for it to look proper. If the camera hasn't moved 35 degrees or more, then it looks like a jump cut. Jump cuts are generally avoided in film, video, and animation. A jump cut is not a seamless transition and can adversely change the flow of a sequence. With that said, a jump cut can also be a useful cut in certain situations. A subject suddenly moving from one part of the frame to another can be confusing to viewers if the movement does not have some logical reason. Jump cuts with characters, products, or location can all be awkward when the movement doesn't make sense. For example, Figure 11.3 shows a framed subject. If the sequence cut to Figure 11.4, you'd be left wondering why the subject suddenly "jumped" across the frame.

11.3 A simple shot with a framed subject.

11.4 A typical jump cut: The same shot, but the subject has instantly changed positions. It is awkward and confusing when not cut together for a specific reason.

A jump cut, however, can work well when the director wants to convey time and space. For example, put Figures 11.3 and 11.4 together with a story that intends to show the expanse of time, and the cut becomes very effective. Another example could be a simple wall clock. For example, your shot shows a character approaching a car parked on a street. Suddenly, the camera is moved up, and the character is standing in front of the car. How did he get there? The shot just "popped" to a different frame. This is a jump cut. As another example of a jump cut is similar to an insert shot. Perhaps your character looks up—you cut to a wall clock. Your goal is to show the subject waiting a long time. Instead of cutting back and forth between the clock, the subject, and the clock, you can use a jump cut to identify a long expanse of time. Keep the shot on the clock with a soft dissolve, perhaps even two or three times. Your viewer sees the clock, then sees it change to a hour later, and then an hour later again. (See Figures 11.5 and 11.6.) Cut back to the subject, and the viewer sees a less-patient character, perhaps now disheveled and irritated.

Another form of a jump cut is a jump-cut sequence. This is a montage sequence in which jump cuts show similar actions or movements happening over a period of time. For example, a scene requires that a frantic burglar searches a room for jewels. A jump-cut sequence could cut between different stages of the robber's mission, each shot showing the next stage of destruction to the room. These jump cuts create a montage

11.5 A shot that has a clock highlights what time it is to the viewer.

11.6 A cut to the same shot, but now with a different time showing, creates an expanse of time for the viewer.

sequence and can actually be very useful. Perhaps you're documenting how a group of people work together to build a house. You can use a jump-cut sequence to show the stages of building and transformation. This scenario makes very good use of a jump-cut sequence because the viewers will see the progress and understand the flow of what they're watching. Simply showing a group of people with piles of material and a framed house, then cutting to a finished house would create a very confusing shot and an inconsistent sequence.

11.1.2 WALK-AND-REVEAL FRAMING

A transition technique, *walk-and-reveal framing*, is an excellent way to identify a subject, then bring the viewer's attention to the subject's interest. While this is often thought of during shooting, it's important to editing. Unless this type of shot is edited together properly, the flow and continuity of the production will be broken. Walk-and-reveal framing starts with a character moving in front of the camera; the viewer sees a partially obscured frame. This allows the editor to cut to a new shot without the viewer noticing. From there, when the character walks out of the frame of view, a different shot is revealed. This technique can be used with characters, cars, animals, or even inanimate objects. Figures 11.7 through 11.9 show a sequence of walk-and-reveal frames.

11.7 An initial shot allows the viewer to see the scene and elements within it.

11.8 Rather than using a jump cut, the director can have a character walk directly in front of the lens of the camera. This allows the editor to cut to a different shot, with the viewer unaware.

11.9 Once the character leaves the frame, the shot has changed, helping keep the flow and continuity of the scene.

A walk-and-reveal frame is an excellent way for a director to keep the viewer's attention on a subject and to avoid a jump cut. Additionally, it avoids a zoom or push-in type shot, which requires more time. Walk-and-reveal framing requires more planning between the director and editor so that the lighting, timing, and subject matter all work well together. As an animator, however, you can create this shot quickly and easily as you design your scenes. In the computer animation environment, you can instantly change lighting and set conditions with a few settings, unlike the traditional filmmaker.

11.1.3 FILL-AND-REVEAL FRAMING

Similar to walk-and-reveal framing in both shooting and editing, the *fill-and-reveal framing* technique involves a subject blocking the lens, which allows the editor to cut the shot without the viewer knowing. However, the fill-and-reveal framing technique uses a moving *camera* rather than a moving subject. For example, a moving camera following a subject might pass a column, or automobile, which temporarily blocks the view. Moments later, after the blocking object is out of frame, the viewer sees a different shot, either within the same scene or not. This technique can work well with two completely different shots if the lens-blocking object is dark and if the motion of the camera going into the edit matches it coming out. Again, like walk-and-reveal framing, this technique takes planning between the editor and director, but it comes more easily to computer animators. You have advantages that traditional filmmakers do not, such as perfect camera timing and quick changes of lenses, focal length, and light. Figures 11.10 through 11.12 show the sequence of shots for a fill-and-reveal framed edit.

11.10 A moving camera follows a subject down a city street.

11.11 As the camera follows the character, it passes behind a beam of the elevated train tracks. Because the camera is focused on the subject across the street, the foreground object that obscures the lens is briefly dark and out of focus, giving the editor and director an opportunity to cut the shot.

11.12 The camera continues its motion following the subject, but when it passes the column on the opposite side, the shot seamlessly changes to a close-up.

You may often see a cut that uses a fill-and-reveal frame to transition to a different scene. Perhaps a car is speeding toward the camera, and just as it fills the frame and obscures the view, the editor cuts to a different scene entirely. (See Figures 11.13 through 11.15.)

11.13 The first shot has a car speeding toward the camera.

11.14 The next shot continues the speeding car toward the camera.

11.15 Just as you think the camera will be smashed with the speeding car, it cuts to an entirely different shot.

11.1.4 FLASH CUTS

You may not be familiar with the term, but you most likely know the technique. *Flash cuts*, or *flashed jump cuts*, are used to simulate a photo flash to add impact to a scene. This editing technique is also used for "flashbacks." For example, a character has been in a terrible car accident and can't remember what happened. As the story unfolds, she begins to recall bits and pieces of the terrible night. To help add impact to the memories and let the viewer know that the subject is remembering, the shots could work like Figures 11.16 and 11.17.

When the shot needs to come back from the memory to the subject, use another flash to white. Audio also is used often to pull the viewer's attention away from the shot. For example, you're focused on a character. A flash of white occurs and the shot cuts to a car accident or perhaps even a childhood memory. The viewer understands what's happening and is not confused. It's clear that this is a memory or thought. To cut back to the present requires an additional flash cut, and the right audio can make it more effective. To draw the subject and viewers back to the present, overlay audio from the upcoming scene, such as the character's friend or spouse calling out. Flash cuts can be used for all types of scenes, from memories to dreams to creative thoughts. This editing technique is an excellent way for you to transition between completely different shots while helping them make sense within the current story.

11.16 A close-up on a character can show the emotion and thought as she begins to remember a terrible car accident.

11.17 A quick flash to white, or perhaps a significant person or incident from the accident, helps the viewer identify the subject's thoughts and memories.

11.1.5 COLLAGES

A *collage* is a great way to add thoughts to a character or idea. They can be used for very soft, dreamlike thoughts or complex, confusing scenes. More than just a split screen with two images, a collage uses multiple images in many places throughout the frame. A collage can be made by simply compositing images over the existing, or base, layer shot, as shown in Figure 11.18.

You can use a collage to blend similar images together or even just to mix different aspects of a shot. For example, your story calls for a scene in which multiple characters are all scrambling to make telephone calls at once. The mood is chaotic, and the shot should represent that. Perhaps there are four people in one house all talking on different phones. A shot of the house with a collage of them each talking on a phone can identify those people and their locations in the house. Add to that audio of their conversations, and your shot becomes a mix of video and audio without a lot of cuts, keeping the mood and feel the director is trying to convey.

11.18 A collage can be edited into a rendered animation to show a character's thoughts or ideas.

11.1.6 SUB-CLIP SHOTS

Similar to a collage, a *sub-clipped shot* adds supporting images to a scene. While a collage uses different shots to bring a scene together, such as a character and a crazy idea, a superimposed shot can be edited together to show what's happening within the same scene. For example, a doctor is looking through a microscope. The director does not want to cut the shot to show what the doctor is looking at through the scope because there is action going on behind him that is important. The editor can add a sub-clip to the shot, which is a superimposed shot of what the doctor is looking at. This editing technique is useful in many areas, such as a group of explorers finding new territory or even a single character looking through a drawer of keepsakes.

> **NOTE**
>
> You may have noticed that many areas of the editing process directly relate to shooting. There is a fine line between the two when describing many of the techniques in this chapter. The goal for you is to understand and employ these techniques whenever appropriate, whether it's during shooting or during the editing session.

11.1.7 SPLIT SCREENS

Split screens are used throughout television and film, especially when identifying two characters talking on the telephone. This technique is useful for showing two separate shots at once. These shots can be interacting, such as two sides of a phone call, or perhaps they are just related. The director might need to tell the story in such a way that the viewer needs to understand that as one element occurs, another is happening at the exact same moment. Spit screens can be vital to a shot if the actions in one shot directly affect the actions in another. A split screen will enable the viewer to understand this.

11.1.8 MONTAGE SEQUENCES

Filmmakers use *montage sequences* to show the passing of time or the progress of an event. You'll most often see them cut to music. Cuts, dissolves, wipes, or even walk-and-reveal edits can be used. Montage sequences are great to use in 3D animation, just as they are film. For example, in the animated movie *Shrek*, the director used a montage sequence when the ogre and his donkey make the journey to save the princess. Instead of wasting the viewers' time creating unnecessary dialogue, he chose to use music and clever animations. A cut from one location to another would seem too quick and abrupt, but animating their journey would take too long.

11.1.9 CUT-ZOOM SHOTS

To help emphasize and add impact to a scene, try a *cut zoom in*. This technique involves quick cuts between a wide, medium, and close-up shot. Typically, a cut zoom in is done with three shots, but two or four can also be used. This is essentially a series of jump cuts, but when put together in this fashion, they work very well as an editing technique. The purpose of this type of edit is to quickly bring the viewer's attention to a specific detail with added interest. For example, a character is startled during a heavy sleep. He sits up quickly, and as he focuses his eyes on the figure that's standing in the doorway, the shots cut from a wide to a medium shot, then to a close-up, and perhaps to an extreme close-up after that. Each shot when cut can be slowly zooming in as well, and each is held for a few seconds only. Figures 11.19 through 11.21 show the three shots.

11.19 To emphasize a shot, the editor uses a cut zoom in series of edits. The first edit is a wide shot of the scene.

11.20 After a few seconds, the editor cuts to a medium shot of the same scene. Each cut also slowly zooms in.

11.21 After a few more seconds, the editor cuts to yet another shot within the same scene, this time to a close-up.

Cut zoom in shots are very effective for dramatic scenes or scenes with a shock value. You can use the opposite technique as well, called a *cut zoom out*. The exact same principles apply, only backward. The editor starts with a close-up, cuts to a medium shot, then wide shot, and sometimes an extreme wide shot. Perhaps you need to show the predicament of a character who's standing alone on a desert highway. He suddenly realizes the intensity of his situation, and to enhance his feelings, the shot can be edited with a cut zoom out. The final shot would show the character as a tiny element in a vast landscape.

11.1.10 MULTI-TAKES

Every once in a while, the action of a single shot is so quick, yet so important, that the director needs to find a way to emphasize it. For example, to emphasize an explosion, the director makes sure that it is shot with multiple cameras or rendered from multiple angles. From there, the editor cuts these multiple angles together as they are happening to create a *multi-take shot*. (See Figures 11.22 through 11.24.)

11.22 The same shot can be used in multiple takes, such as from a bystander point of view.

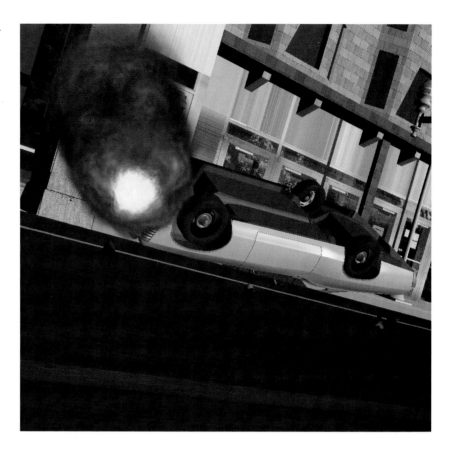

11.23 A quick take to an overhead shot of the same scene adds interest.

11.24 Another cut to a wide shot emphasizes the scene.

11.1.11 CUT-AWAY SHOTS

Cut-away shots are extremely useful in editing. The editor uses a cut-away to transition between awkward shots or difficult camera changes. When you edit your animation together, you don't want to keep the shot on the same subject all the time. Editing in a cut-away will break the monotony and add interest to your production. In addition, cut-aways are useful as reaction shots and simply to cover up mistakes. For example, the camera is following the dialogue of two lovers. The man needs to explain his feelings to the woman and then propose marriage. During his dialogue, there is an awkward fumble as he reaches for his ring. Because the director created a close-up shot of the man reaching for the woman's hand, the editor can use that shot as a cut-away. He'll hold on it for a few seconds, then cut back to the dialogue, at which point the man now has the ring in his hand and is ready to take that big leap.

In animation, your cut-aways might be used differently. In animation, you're not relying on live actors who can make mistakes, but rather, you have the tools to make an entire sequence perfect. If you were animating a marriage proposal, you might still use a cut-away to the man reaching for the woman's hand—not to cover up an awkward grab for the ring in a pocket, but to add more emotion. Additionally, a cut-away avoids a jump cut. For example, the dialogue of the man and woman as the proposal starts is a medium shot of the two. You want to move in closer to an over-the-shoulder shot. A cut-away will allow you to make that transition flow.

11.1.12 LOOK-AT EDITS

Generally, look-at shots and edits involve a character and his reaction. *Look-at edits* are good to use during your edit session, as they involve a character looking at something, a cut-shot to what he's looking at, then a shot of his reaction. While you might not think this is anything more than a cut-away, the look-at can be significant to the viewer's understanding of a character's feelings. Consider, for example, an old woman sitting near the man who is proposing marriage. Your first shot of the old woman shows a sad and lonely face. She glances to her left—the shot cuts to the man proposing to the woman—cut back to the woman to show her reaction, which is a warm smile. You understand that although she might be lonely, that moment may have reminded her of her own marriage proposal so many years ago. The order of the look-at edit is important here. Imagine if the sequence were cut together wrongly. First, the old woman has the warm smile, she looks to her left to see the marriage proposal, and when the shot cuts back, she is now sad and lonely. Taken this way, the mood is entirely different and perhaps can tell a different story—all from the way a shot is cut together.

11.1.13 FREEZE FRAMES

Freeze frames are not often thought of for 3D animation, but there's no reason you shouldn't use this editing technique in your animation projects. A *freeze frame* is a single frame held for a length of time to add emphasis to an image. An example of where a freeze frame might be used is a boxing match. Perhaps your character has been beaten down but ends up winning the bout with a knock-out punch. You can use a freeze frame of the final punch to emphasize the importance of the shot. Freeze frames in editing are mostly a style and are not always necessary.

11.1.14 CROSS-CUT EDITS

If you have an animation that is very suspenseful or dramatic, a *cross-cut edit* can be used. A cross-cut edit is used to show parallel actions in two places. It is interspersing shots of each scene taking place simultaneously. You also can use cross-cuts to emphasize a scene in which multiple events are happening. An innocent deer is grazing for food in the woods, for instance, and the shot is peaceful and steady. Cut to a fast-paced, raging tiger quickly approaching the unassuming deer. Suspense mounts as the cuts between the two shots become quicker, inevitably ending with the tiger and deer in the same shot.

11.1.15 MATCH CUTS

Match cuts are very precise and should be done without notice. That is to say, unlike a jump cut that is very obvious, a match cut should be seamless. The transition between one shot and another should go unnoticed by the viewer. Action sequences are excellent candidates for match-cut editing. When the action happens, the shot cuts. The result is that viewers don't notice the transition, but rather, focus on the action. Match cuts are also good edits for dialogue or character animation. For example, a character sits up and looks off camera, and the shot cuts to where the character is looking. This transition is natural, as you expect to see what the character sees. If the shot is held too long or not cut on the shift of the eyes, the viewer can begin to wonder what the character is looking at.

11.1.16 SUBLIMINAL CUTS

Filmmakers can add *subliminal cuts* in films to influence the viewer. A quick few-frame cuts to a different image can go almost unnoticed, but can trigger the viewer's subconscious. A subliminal cut is often considered a message to the viewer, such as in a horror film when the main character has visions of death. A quick flash of the grim reaper can send a message to the viewer that the end is near for the character. (See Figures 11.25 through 11.27.)

11.25 An initial shot of a character is relatively standard.

11.26 While watching the sequence, a few frames of a skull are cut into the shot, barely noticeable by the viewer.

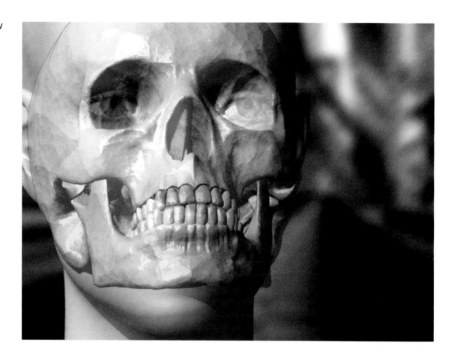

11.27 The shot cuts back to the character whose expression has now changed after the subliminal shot is cut in.

11.1.17 SLOW MOTION

Slow motion can extend the length of a shot and add impact to a sequence. When action is played out slowly, viewers have time to take in what they're seeing, such as in a huge explosion scene. When tied with music, slow motion shots are often excellent for conveying strong emotion.

Now, you don't often render animations in slow motion, although it's not a bad idea. You can do this by simply scaling the entire animation in time. For example, perhaps you created a three-second animation of a boy jumping off of a building. The shot is good, but now a slow-motion shot is needed. If you scale the entire animation by 100, you can render the animation in slow motion. But in most cases, animators render out their scenes as they normally would and, in editing, slow the shots to a desired speed. However, time-scaling your animation can produce a very cool result.

In film, directors and cinematographers specifically design shots for slow motion by filming at more than 24 frames per second. When the high-speed film is played back at its normal frame rate, a slow-motion effect is achieved. This is called a planned shot. For 3D animators, slow motion can be achieved simply with the push of a button in your favorite nonlinear editing software or by time scaling as mentioned above.

11.1.18 FAST MOTION

If a filmmaker can achieve a slow motion planned shot by shooting film at more than 24 frames per second, it's possible to achieve fast motion by shooting at less than 24 frames per second. Again, you can achieve this through your digital editing program or by time scaling your animation. The purpose of *fast motion shots* in editing is to create a desired effect. Many films today use fast motion shots to quickly move the camera from one location to another, which helps set the pace of the scene. Directors consider these post-production techniques as early as pre-production so that shots are designed around them. You should be aware of the techniques you can employ and work toward them throughout your production.

11.1.19 EYE JOURNEYS

A great editing technique that you can easily use in 3D animation is a *journey through the eye*. Perhaps your character has far-off ideas or you need to convey a dreamlike thought. You can zoom or push the camera into the character's eye, which then cuts to a completely different scene. The goal to have the viewer travel into the mind of the character. You can cut or dissolve these shots together to create this effect. What you're conveying to the viewer with this technique is the character's thoughts. (See Figures 11.28 through 11.30.)

11.28 To see a character's thoughts, you can begin an edit by showing a close-up of the character's face.

11.29 You can cut or dissolve to a close-up shot of the character's eyes to bring the viewer closer into her thoughts.

11.30 Go one step further, and cut or dissolve to an extreme close-up shot of the character's eyes. This really brings the viewer into her subconscious.

11.1.20 SLICE OF LIFE

Slice of life is probably one of the most over-used effects in editing today. For this technique, which can also be called *bullet time*, a series of cameras is set up around a character or action to take sequential pictures with a slight offset. Those images are put into a computer and compiled to make a complete shot. You'll often see this technique in fight sequences. For example, a character jumps up in the air to do a high kick to his opponent. The shot slows down significantly and then pans all the way around the character, who seems suspended in time. Although this is a difficult process for traditional filmmakers, it's quite easy for 3D animators to set up. One way to achieve this look in animation is to simply freeze your character's motions, but keep the camera moving. The addition of a motion blur helps sell the effect.

NOTE

When creating a slice of life or bullet time effect, your character will have no inherent motion blur. To set up this type of effect properly, make sure your character's motion is oscillating between half frames in order to preserve the self-motion blur.

11.1.21 GLOBAL ZOOMS

It seems that clients always want this type of shot. A *global zoom* is a shot that starts in outer space and zooms all the way down to Earth to a specific house, car, or character. These shots are edited together in pieces to appear seamless. The trick to editing these shots together is to move the camera at a constant rate and to use atmosphere and cloud layers as soft transitions between levels.

For example, the shot opens in outer space, with the viewer looking at the Earth. The shot zooms in, and as the Earth fills the frame, an atmosphere layer quickly dissolves up, then the shot dissolves to a shot of a large land expanse. The viewer just traveled from outer space into the Earth's atmosphere and never realized there was a transition. As the camera zooms in, another animated atmosphere or cloud layer can be used as a transition to a closer shot, such as a neighborhood. From there, another transition can take place, and the shot can then show a close-up of the character or subject. These quick transitions at a constant speed are edited together to create a seamless flow that creates a truly global shot. Conversely, the shots can be rendered and edited together to pull toward outer space from ground level. Even though a shot like this is easier in the computer environment than the traditional world, the editing of transitional layers can significantly help your production workflow. Instead of modeling miles of buildings and streets, a fast-moving camera transitioned through clouds can mask a shot and eliminates the need for additional rendering.

11.31 Global shots can start either on Earth or in space. Here, a shot begins in outer space, looking at the Earth, and it begins a fast zoom in.

11.32 Rather than modeling and animating unnecessary models and elements, transitional layers of clouds and atmospheres are edited together to move from one shot to the next.

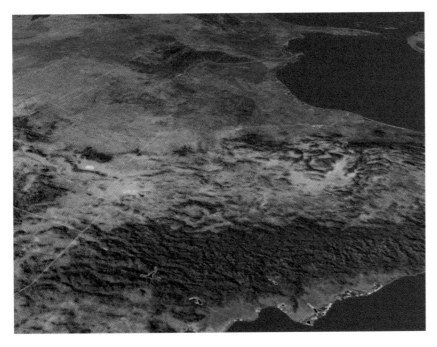

11.33 After a cloud layer transition, the edit shows a closer view of the Earth. Played together, the edits create one long global zoom.

11.2 PARTING SHOTS

The goal of this chapter was to introduce you to common techniques editors use to bring shots together. Understanding these techniques can help you plan better, from pre-production through modeling, animating, and even rendering. Remember, you should use editing to finish your animated films—not to fix them.

Editing is an art form all its own. It is sometimes a thankless job, but without it, a film, video, or animation is nothing more than a grocery bag of ingredients. Although editing is a highly respected art, it's often thought of last in many animation studios. Think of editing as part of the entire cinematic and directorial process! The right combination of transitions, cuts, and dissolves, combined with the proper time, create the gourmet meal. Editing is more than cutting shots together and adding sound. It is the finishing, the polish, and the glue that brings your story together.

CHAPTER 12

FINAL THOUGHTS

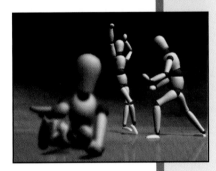

C HECK OUT THE FILM and television section of any bookstore, and you'll find lots of books about cinematography, directing, writing, camera basics, and much more. Specifically for animators, *[digital] Cinematography and Directing* was written to compliment those books, but also to take you closer to the type of animation and imaging possible in 3D. The intent behind this guide was not to bore you with technical jargon or lengthy charts and comparisons. Rather, through clear examples and 3D illustrations, to let you see first hand how proper cameras, lenses, staging, and more can be used to make your projects even better. Here is a list of resources you can use for even more technical and specific cinematic information:

- *CG 101: A Computer Graphics Industry Reference*. By Terrence Masson. New Riders Publishing, 1999. ISBN: 073570046X.

- *Filmmaker's Dictionary, 2ⁿᵈ Edition*. By Ralph S. Singleton. Lone Eagle Publishing, 2000. ISBN: 1580650228.

- *From Word to Image: Storyboarding and the Filmmaking Process*. By Marcie Begleiter. Michael Wiese Productions, 2001. ISBN: 0941188280.

- *Learning to Light: Easy and Affordable Techniques for the Photographer*. By Roger Hicks and Frances Schultz. Amphoto Books, 1998. ISBN: 0817441794.

- *Making Movies Work: Thinking Like a Filmmaker.* By Jon Boorstin. Silman-James Press, 1995. ISBN: 1879505274.

- *Storyboarding 101: A Crash Course in Professional Storyboarding.* By James O. Fraioli. Michael Wiese Productions, 2000. ISBN: 0941188256.

- *Visual Effects Cinematography.* By Zoran Perisic. Focal Press, 2000. ISBN: 0240803515.

As you've seen throughout these chapters, many traditional principles of real-world photography, filmmaking, lighting, and directing translate to the 3D digital world. There is more to creating within the computer environment, however, than copying values or mimicking techniques. Techniques such as these could be used for crazy alien or robot animations, or animated particles for ghosts, or water coming to life. Computer animation can be whatever you want it to be. To this end, this book has taken you from digital cinematography basics to directing methods to rendering using a short animation project of a city street and other examples.

12.1 WHERE YOU'VE BEEN

The book started by discussing the foundations of filmmaking: Lenses, f-stops, and apertures are as much a part of 3D as they are in the real world. At least, they should be! Most 3D applications give you the tools to create a real-world camera from depth of field settings to exposures. Refer to these early chapters often to remind yourself of the benefits of lenses and f-stops.

As the book progressed, you learned that storyboarding and planning can significantly increase your productivity. Even simple stick figures allow you to pre-visualize your shots and any necessary elements that might need to be modeled or added to your scenes. Planning in 3D is as important as it is in the traditional world, with its own variations.

Camera angles and staging are key to establishing the best possible shots in your animations. Your advantage in the computer environment is that you can instantly make changes. While you might have a producer or client to answer to, there are no physical limitations to changing shots, as there are in the traditional filmmaking world. Additionally, you don't have to worry about your actors perfecting their actions and dialogues a second and third time while you perfect just the right camera move. Your actors are digital, as are your lights, which allows you to focus your attention elsewhere.

Animators often jump right in and begin modeling and animating. It isn't until later that they worry about resolutions and rendering. But, as the latter part of this book discussed, setting the right resolution can play a role in the types of shots you end up with and how much detail your 3D scene needs, or more importantly, doesn't need.

12.2 YOUR NEXT STEP

With traditional cinematic principles applied, your animations can come to life. I've recommended before that you watch the big boys for ideas, and I can't stress this enough. Watch what the major studios are doing, and do it yourself on your computer. One of the best ways to create more cinematic images yourself is to watch the behind-the-scenes features provided with almost every movie on DVD. Listen to the issues that the director and effects artists had to overcome. Pay close attention to the series of shots the artists used to make a final sequence. How was it lit? What sort of real-world and digital elements were involved? There are many great movies on DVD that have hours of behind-the-scenes info such as *Forrest Gump, Apollo 13, The Lord of the Rings, A Beautiful Mind*, and *Fight Club*. These, as well as hundreds of other DVDs, can provide you with not only great information, but great ideas!

You may hear companies brag that their software will allow you to make your own movies right at home. You know what? They're right! You have what you need to create your own digital movie, no matter what your software. Animators who started on very slow systems like Pentium 75s or Amigas understood and knew how to be creative with the tools they had. You, the modern-day animator, shouldn't sweat the fact that you "only" have a 400Mhz machine or "just" 256MB of memory. Sure, a top-of-the-line machine loaded to the max with RAM would be great, but don't let that stop you. Nothing should stop your creativity and drive to create the next great 3D animation.

I hope you learned that the camera in 3D is an extremely valuable tool, and that planning and direction are as much a part of 3D as the models and animation themselves. Always take pictures, and always take video, as you can continually develop your eye. Don't stop experimenting, don't stop learning, and soon you'll be accepting your Oscar! Oh, and when you do win, invite me to the party.

INDEX

Peachpit
Essential books for the creative community

Visit Peachpit on the Web at www.peachpit.com

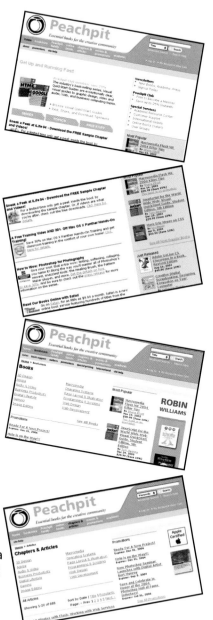

- Read the latest articles and download timesaving tipsheets from best-selling authors such as Scott Kelby, Robin Williams, Lynda Weinman, Ted Landau, and more!

- Join the Peachpit Club and save 25% off all your online purchases at peachpit.com every time you shop—plus enjoy free UPS ground shipping within the United States.

- Search through our entire collection of new and upcoming titles by author, ISBN, title, or topic. There's no easier way to find just the book you need.

- Sign up for newsletters offering special Peachpit savings and new book announcements so you're always the first to know about our newest books and killer deals.

- Did you know that Peachpit also publishes books by Apple, New Riders, Adobe Press, Macromedia Press, palmOne Press, and TechTV press? Swing by the Peachpit family section of the site and learn about all our partners and series.

- Got a great idea for a book? Check out our About section to find out how to submit a proposal. You could write our next best-seller!

You'll find all this and more at www.peachpit.com. Stop by and take a look today!

VISIT OUR WEB SITE

WWW.NEWRIDERS.COM

On our web site, you'll find information about our other books, authors, tables of contents, and book errata. You will also find information about book registration and how to purchase our books, both domestically and internationally.

EMAIL US

Contact us at: **nrfeedback@newriders.com**

- If you have comments or questions about this book
- To report errors that you have found in this book
- If you have a book proposal to submit or are interested in writing for New Riders
- If you are an expert in a computer topic or technology and are interested in being a technical editor who reviews manuscripts for technical accuracy

Contact us at: **nreducation@newriders.com**

- If you are an instructor from an educational institution who wants to preview New Riders books for classroom use. Email should include your name, title, school, department, address, phone number, office days/hours, text in use, and enrollment, along with your request for desk/examination copies and/or additional information.

Contact us at: **nrmedia@newriders.com**

- If you are a member of the media who is interested in reviewing copies of New Riders books. Send your name, mailing address, and email address, along with the name of the publication or web site you work for.

BULK PURCHASES/CORPORATE SALES

The publisher offers discounts on this book when ordered in quantity for bulk purchases and special sales. For sales within the U.S., please contact: Corporate and Government Sales (800) 382-3419 or **corpsales@pearsontechgroup.com**. Outside of the U.S., please contact: International Sales (317) 581-3793 or **international@pearsontechgroup.com**.

WRITE TO US

New Riders Publishing
201 W. 103rd St.
Indianapolis, IN 46290-1097

CALL/FAX US

Toll-free (800) 571-5840
If outside U.S. (317) 581-3500
Ask for New Riders
FAX: (317) 581-4663

New Riders

WWW.NEWRIDERS.COM

VOICES THAT MATTER

OUR AUTHORS

PRESS ROOM

| ::: web development | ::: design | ::: photoshop | ::: new media | ::: 3-D | ::: server technologies |

EDUCATORS

ABOUT US

CONTACT US

You already know that New Riders brings you the **Voices that Matter**.

But what does that mean? It means that New Riders brings you the

Voices that challenge your assumptions, take your talents to the next

level, or simply help you better understand the complex technical world

we're all navigating.

Visit **www.newriders.com** to find:

- ▶ **10% discount** and **free shipping** on all book purchases
- ▶ Never before published chapters
- ▶ Sample chapters and excerpts
- ▶ Author bios and interviews
- ▶ Contests and enter-to-wins
- ▶ Up-to-date industry event information
- ▶ Book reviews
- ▶ Special offers from our friends and partners
- ▶ Info on how to join our User Group program
- ▶ Ways to have your Voice heard

New
Riders

WWW.NEWRIDERS.COM